Make 'em Happy. Fix it Fast!

BUSY WOMAN'S Quick & Easy Recipes

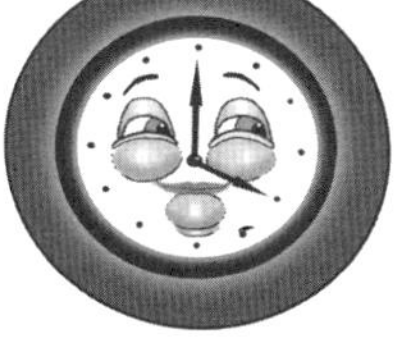

hinkler

Published by Hinkler Books Pty Ltd 2011
45–55 Fairchild Street
Heatherton Victoria 3202 Australia
www.hinkler.com.au

Illustration: Nancy Bohanan
Prepress: Splitting Image
Typesetting: MPS Limited

ISBN: 978 1 7418 4087 2

Printed and bound in China

BUSY WOMAN'S
Quick & Easy Recipes

Busy woman ... kind of redundant, isn't it?

What woman isn't busy? Look around, can you find one? We couldn't either. ***Busy Woman's Quick and Easy Recipes*** is a collection of time-saving meal ideas that will actually give busy women the opportunity to scratch one thing off that to-do list each day.

These recipes were tested for taste and ease of preparation right in our own kitchens. From appetisers to mains and soups to desserts, this cookbook is filled with excellent meal ideas that are simple enough for the busiest of people.

We didn't just think about getting dinner together. We looked at the whole picture. If a meal made a big mess in our kitchen, it didn't make the cookbook. If we couldn't locate the ingredients at our local supermarket, we didn't include them. These recipes are simple from start to finish without sacrificing one bit of flavour.

After all, a few minutes saved in the kitchen are a few more minutes to spend with your family. And that is time well spent.

CONTENTS

CONTENTS

There is a time every day when the phones are quiet, TV is off and emails will wait until later.

For a few moments, you are not a student or an executive; at a meeting or on a sales call.

For this short time, you are family.

This is dinner time.

APPETISERS

Fiesta Dip

1 (15 ounce) can refried beans	425 g
1 (16 ounce) can chilli without beans	.5 kg
1 cup salsa	240 ml
8 ounce sharp cheddar cheese, shredded	225 g
1 cup finely chopped onion	240 ml

- Mash beans with fork.
- In saucepan, combine all ingredients and heat to mix.
- Serve hot with biscuits (crackers) or corn (tortilla) chips.

Onion-Guacamole Dip

1 (8 ounce) carton sour cream	225 g
1 (1 ounce) packet dry onion soup mix	30 g
2 (8 ounce) cartons prepared avocado dip	2 (225 g)
2 spring (green) onions with tops, chopped	
½ teaspoon crushed dill	2 ml

- Mix all ingredients and chill.
- Serve with corn (tortilla) chips.

Crunchy Asparagus Dip

14 ounce asparagus, chopped	395 g
½ cup mayonnaise	120 ml
¼ teaspoon chilli (hot) sauce	1 ml
½ cup chopped pecans	120 ml

- Combine all ingredients in medium bowl and chill.
- Serve with biscuits (crackers).

Hot Broccoli Dip

2 pounds processed cheese, cubed	1 kg
1 (10 ounce) can mushroom soup	280 g
10 ounce broccoli, chopped	280 g
Chilli powder to taste	

- In saucepan, melt cheese with soup and stir in broccoli and chilli powder.
- Heat thoroughly.
- Serve hot with corn (tortilla) chips.

Horsey Dip

8 ounce cream cheese, softened	225 g
⅔ cup mayonnaise	160 ml
1 tablespoon lemon juice	15 ml
3 tablespoons creamy horseradish	45 ml
¼ cup chilli sauce	60 ml
¼ teaspoon garlic powder	1 ml
16 ounce cooked prawns (shrimp)	450 g
2 spring (green) onions with tops, chopped	

- In mixing bowl, combine cream cheese, mayonnaise, lemon juice, horseradish, chilli sauce and garlic powder and blend well.
- Remove the head and shell, and chop prawns (shrimp) and onions, add to cream cheese mixture, blend and chill. Serve with corn (tortilla) chips.

Hot Sombrero Dip

2 (15 ounce) cans refried beans	2 (425 g)
1 pound lean beef mince (ground beef), cooked	.5 kg
4 ounce green chillies	115 g
1 cup hot salsa	240 ml
1½ cups processed cheese, shredded	360 ml

- Preheat oven to 180° C (350° F).
- Layer bean dip, beef, chillies and salsa in 3-litre (3-quart) baking dish and top with cheese.
- Bake just until cheese melts, about 10 or 15 minutes.
- Serve with corn (tortilla) chips.

Vegetable Dip

1 (10 ounce) package frozen chopped spinach, thawed, well drained	280 g
1 bunch spring (green) onions with tops, chopped	
1 (1 ounce) packet dry vegetable soup mix	30 g
1 tablespoon lemon juice	15 ml
16 ounce sour cream	450 g

- Squeeze spinach in paper towels to drain thoroughly.
- In medium bowl, combine all ingredients and add a little salt. (Adding several drops of chilli (hot) sauce is also good.)
- Cover and refrigerate. Serve with corn (tortilla) chips.

Velvet Clam Dip

11 ounce cream cheese	310 g
¼ cup butter	60 ml
2 (6 ounce) cans minced clams, drained (alternatively use another canned seafood)	2 (170 g)
½ teaspoon Worcestershire sauce	2 ml

- Melt cream cheese and butter in bain-marie (double boiler).
- Add minced clams and Worcestershire sauce.
- Serve hot.

Chunky Shrimp Dip

2 (6 ounce) cans tiny, cooked shrimp, drained	2 (170 g)
2 cups mayonnaise	480 ml
6 spring (green) onions with tops, finely chopped	
¾ cup chunky salsa	180 ml

- Crumble shrimp and stir in mayonnaise, onion and salsa.
- Chill for 1 to 2 hours.
- Serve with biscuits (crackers).

Hot Rich Crab Dip

1 (10 ounce) packet processed cheese spread	280 g
1 (16 ounce) processed cheese, cubed with chopped jalapeño chillies	.5 kg
1 (6 ounce) can crabmeat, flaked, drained	170 g
1 (16 ounce) jar salsa	.5 kg

- In microwave-safe bowl, combine cheese spread and cubed cheese.
- Microwave at 1-minute intervals until cheese melts.
- Add crabmeat and salsa and mix well.
- Serve hot with corn (tortilla) chips.

Unbelievable Crab Dip

Don't count on your guests leaving the table until this dip is gone!

16 ounce processed cheese, cubed	.5 kg
2 (6 ounce) cans crabmeat, drained, flaked	2 (170 g)
1 bunch spring (green) onions with tops, chopped	
2 cups mayonnaise	480 ml
½ teaspoon seasoned salt	2 ml

- Melt cheese in top of bain-marie (double boiler). Add crabmeat, onions, mayonnaise and seasoned salt.
- Serve hot or at room temperature with assorted biscuits (crackers).

Tasty Tuna Dip

1 (6 ounce) can tuna in spring water, drained, flaked	170 g
1 (1 ounce) packet salad dressing mix	30 g
1 (8 ounce) carton sour cream	225 g
¼ cup chopped black olives, drained	60 ml

- Combine all ingredients and stir until they blend.
- Chill for 8 hours. Serve with Melba toast.

Hot Artichoke Spread

1 (14 ounce) can artichoke hearts, drained, chopped	395 g
1 (4 ounce) can chopped green chillies, drained	115 g
1 cup mayonnaise	240 ml
1 cup mozzarella cheese, shredded	240 ml
¼ teaspoon white pepper	1 ml
½ teaspoon garlic salt	2 ml
Paprika	

- Preheat oven to 150° C (300° F).
- Remove any spikes or tough leaves from artichoke hearts. Combine all ingredients and mix well.
- Place in sprayed 23-cm (9-inch) baking dish and sprinkle paprika over top.
- Bake for 30 minutes. Serve warm with corn (tortilla) chips or biscuits (crackers).

Creamy Ham Dip

This will also make great little sandwiches on rye bread.

16 ounce cream cheese, softened	**(450 g)**
2 (6 ounce) cans devilled ham	**2 (170 g)**
2 heaped tablespoons horseradish	**30 ml**
¼ cup onion, minced	**60 ml**
¼ cup celery, finely chopped	**60 ml**

- In mixing bowl, beat cream cheese until creamy.
- Stir in ham, horseradish, onion and celery.
- Chill and serve with biscuits (crackers).

Nutty Apple Dip

8 ounce cream cheese, softened	**225 g**
1 cup brown sugar	**240 ml**
1 teaspoon vanilla extract	**5 ml**
1 cup pecans, finely chopped	**240 ml**

- In small mixing bowl combine cream cheese, sugar and vanilla and beat until smooth.
- Stir in pecans. Serve with sliced apples for dipping.

Zippy Broccoli-Cheese Dip

10 ounce broccoli, chopped	280 g
2 tablespoons butter	30 ml
2 sticks celery, chopped	
1 small onion, finely chopped	
16 ounce cheese, cubed processed with chopped jalapeño chillies	.5 kg

- Place butter in large saucepan and saute broccoli, celery and onion at medium heat for about 5 minutes. Stir several times.
- Add cheese. Heat just until cheese melts and stir constantly.
- Serve hot with corn (tortilla) chips.

TIP: If you want the 'zip' to be zippier, add extra jalapeño chillies.

Tuna Melt Appetiser

1 (10 ounce) package frozen spinach, drained	280 g
2 (6 ounce) cans tuna in water, drained, flaked	2 (170 g)
¾ cup mayonnaise	180 ml
1½ cups mozzarella cheese, shredded, divided	360 ml

- Preheat oven to 180° C (350° F).
- Squeeze spinach in several paper towels to drain thoroughly.
- In large bowl, combine spinach, tuna, mayonnaise and 1 cup (240 ml) cheese and mix well.
- Spoon into sprayed pie dish and bake for 15 minutes.
- Remove from oven and sprinkle remaining cheese over top.
- Return to oven and bake for additional 5 minutes.
- Serve with biscuits (crackers).

Hot Cocktail Squares

4 ounce green chillies, chopped	**115 g**
3 ounce bacon bits	**85 g**
16 ounce cheddar cheese, shredded	**.5 kg**
7 eggs	

- Preheat oven to 180° C (350° F).
- In sprayed 18 x 28-cm (7 x 11-inch) baking dish, layer green chillies, bacon bits and cheese.
- Beat eggs well with fork and season with a little salt and several drops chilli (hot) sauce. Pour over cheese and bake covered for 25 minutes.
- Uncover and bake additional 10 minutes. Cut into squares and serve warm.

Walnut-Cheese Spread

¾ cup chopped walnuts	**180 ml**
16 ounce cheddar cheese, shredded	**.5 kg**
3 spring (green) onions with tops, chopped	
½–¾ cup mayonnaise	**120 ml**
½ teaspoon smoky barbecue sauce	**2 ml**

- Roast walnuts at 120° C (250° F) for 10 minutes.
- Combine all ingredients and let stand in refrigerator overnight.
- Spread on assorted biscuits (crackers).

Speedy Chilli Con Queso

16 ounce processed cheese, cubed	.5 kg
½ cup milk	120 ml
1 (12 ounce) jar salsa, divided	340 g

- Melt cheese and milk in bain-marie (double boiler).
- Add about half of salsa. Taste and add more salsa as needed for desired heat.
- Serve with corn (tortilla) chips.

Sausage-Pineapple Bits

This 'sweet and hot' combination has a delicious flavour.

1 pound sausages, cooked, skinned	.5 kg
1 pound spicy sausage meat	.5 kg
1 (15 ounce) can crushed pineapple with juice	425 g
2 cups brown sugar	480 ml
1 tablespoon Worcestershire sauce with a dash of white wine added	15 ml

- Slice sausage into .8-cm (⅓-inch) pieces. Shape sausage meat into 2.5-cm (1-inch) balls.
- In frying pan (skillet), brown sausage balls.
- In large saucepan, combine pineapple, brown sugar and Worcestershire. Heat, add sausages and simmer for 30 minutes.
- Serve from chafing dish or small slow cooker with cocktail toothpicks.

Party Smokies

1 cup tomato sauce (ketchup)	240 ml
1 cup plum jam (jelly)	240 ml
1 tablespoon lemon juice	15 ml
4 tablespoons mustard	60 ml
10 ounce tiny smoked sausages	(290 g)

- In saucepan, combine tomato sauce (ketchup), jam (jelly), lemon juice and mustard, heat and mix well.
- Add sausages and simmer for 10 minutes.
- Serve hot with cocktail toothpicks.

Sausage Bites

1 pound spicy sausages	.5 kg
1 pound cheddar cheese, shredded	.5 kg
3¾ cups scone (biscuit) mix	890 ml
½ teaspoon crushed garlic	2 ml

- Preheat oven to 180° C (350° F).
- Combine all ingredients and knead thoroughly.
- Roll into 2.5-cm (1-inch) balls.
- Bake on baking tray (sheet) for 15 to 18 minutes or until light brown.

Spinach-Artichoke Dip

2 (10 ounce) packages frozen spinach, thawed, drained	2 (280 g)
1 (14 ounce) jar marinated artichoke hearts, drained, finely chopped	395 g
1 cup mayonnaise	240 ml
2 cups mozzarella cheese, shredded	480 ml

- Squeeze spinach in paper towels to drain thoroughly.
- Combine all ingredients and mix well.
- Cover and chill.
- Serve with corn (tortilla) chips.

Olive-Cheese Balls

2¼ cups sharp cheddar cheese, shredded	540 ml
1 cup plain (all-purpose) flour	240 ml
½ cup butter, melted	120 ml
1 (5 ounce) jar green olives	145 g

- Preheat oven to 180° C (350° F).
- In large bowl, combine cheese and flour. Add butter and mix well.
- Cover olives with mixture and form into balls.
- Bake for about 15 minutes or until light brown.

Creamy Spinach-Chilli Dip

1 (10 ounce) package frozen chopped spinach, drained	280 g
8 ounce cheddar cheese, shredded	225 g
8 ounce cream cheese, softened	225 g
1–2 tablespoons chopped jalapeños	15 ml

- Drain spinach several times, wrap in paper towels and squeeze remaining liquid from spinach.
- Combine spinach, cheddar, cream cheese and jalapeños in microwave-safe bowl and heat in microwave on medium until cheese melts. Stir several times while heating.
- Serve hot with corn (tortilla) chips or biscuits (crackers).

To quickly slice mushrooms, small tomatoes, radishes and similar firm fruits and vegetables, use an egg slicer.

Creamy Onion Dip

16 ounce cream cheese, softened	(450 g)
3 tablespoons lemon juice	45 ml
1 (1 ounce) packet dry onion soup mix	30 g
1 (8 ounce) carton sour cream	225 g

- Use mixer to beat cream cheese until smooth.
- Add lemon juice and soup mix. Gradually fold in sour cream and blend well.
- Chill and serve with chips, biscuits (crackers) or fresh vegetables.

Favourite Stand-By Shrimp Dip

2 cups tiny, cooked shrimp, finely chopped	480 ml
2 tablespoons horseradish	30 ml
½ cup chilli sauce	120 ml
¾ cup mayonnaise	180 ml
1 tablespoon lemon juice	15 ml

- Combine all ingredients with a few dashes salt and refrigerate. (If shrimp has been frozen, be sure to drain well.)
- Serve with cucumber or zucchini (courgette) slices.

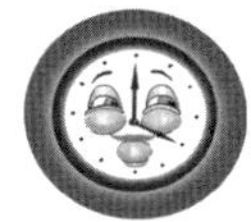

Crab Dip Kick

8 ounce cream cheese, softened	**225 g**
3 tablespoons salsa	**45 ml**
2 tablespoons horseradish	**30 ml**
1 (6 ounce) can crabmeat, drained, flaked	**170 g**

- In mixing bowl, beat cream cheese until creamy.
- Add salsa and horseradish and mix well.
- Stir in crabmeat and refrigerate.
- Serve with assorted biscuits (crackers).

Creamy Cucumber Spread

8 ounce cream cheese, softened	**225 g**
½ cup mayonnaise	**120 ml**
1 teaspoon seasoned salt	**5 ml**
1 cup cucumbers, seeded, chopped	**240 ml**

- With mixer, beat cream cheese until creamy and add mayonnaise, seasoned salt and cucumber.
- Spread on biscuits (crackers).

Reuse those holiday tins. Once the biscuits (cookies) are all gone, use the colourful tins to store baking items and accessories, such as all those tools you used to decorate that cake – five years ago.

Roasted Garlic Dip

4–5 whole garlic cloves with peel	
16 ounce cream cheese, softened	450 g
¾ cup mayonnaise	180 ml
1 (7 or 9 ounce) jar roasted sweet red capsicum (peppers), drained, coarsely chopped	200 g
1 bunch spring (green) onions with tops, chopped	

- Preheat oven to 200° C (400° F).
- Lightly brush outside of garlic cloves with a little oil and place in shallow baking pan.
- Heat about 10 minutes and cool.
- Press roasted garlic out of cloves.
- Beat cream cheese and mayonnaise until creamy. Add garlic, red capsicum (peppers) and onions and mix well. (Roasted capsicums are great in this recipe, but if you want it a little spicy, add several drops of chilli sauce.)
- Sprinkle with paprika and serve with chips or biscuits (crackers).

BEVERAGES

Cranberry-Pineapple Punch

46 ounce cranberry juice	1.4 L
46 ounce pineapple juice	1.4 L
½ cup sugar	120 ml
2 teaspoons almond extract	10 ml
2 quarts ginger ale, chilled	2 L

- Combine cranberry juice, pineapple juice, sugar and almond extract and stir until sugar dissolves. Cover and chill 8 hours.
- When ready to serve, add ginger ale and stir.

Best Tropical Punch

46 ounce pineapple juice	1.4 L
46 ounce apricot nectar	1.4 L
18 ounce lime juice cordial (frozen limeaid concentrate, thawed)	530 ml
3 quarts ginger ale, chilled	3 L

- Combine pineapple juice, apricot nectar and cordial (limeaid concentrate) and chill.
- When ready to serve, add ginger ale.

Sparkling Ginger Punch

750 ml sparkling wine, chilled	
32 ounce ginger ale, chilled	950 ml
6 ounce orange juice cordial (concentrate)	180 ml
Orange slices, optional	

- Combine sparkling wine, ginger ale and orange juice cordial (concentrate) in punch bowl and mix well.
- Serve chilled and garnish with orange slices.

Orange Slush

2 cups orange juice	480 ml
½ cup instant, non-fat milk powder	120 ml
¼ teaspoon almond extract	1 ml
8 ice cubes	

- Combine all ingredients in blender and process on high until mixture is smooth and thick.
- Serve immediately.

If you need a quick festive punch or a special, celebratory drink, sparkling wine and canned fruit juices can save the day. Choose tropical flavours or bright colours. Mix two parts sparkling wine and one or two parts juice and you have a beautiful, delightful drink in just a few minutes.

Lemon-Banana Shake

6 ounce lemon juice cordial (concentrate)	180 ml
1 cup bananas, diced	240 ml
1 quart vanilla ice-cream	1 L
3 cups milk	710 ml

- In mixing bowl, combine cordial (concentrate) and bananas and beat until mixture is thick.
- For each milkshake, add 1 scoop vanilla ice-cream and ¼ cup (60 ml) lemon-banana mixture in glass.
- Fill glass two-thirds with milk and stir well.
- Top off with 1 more scoop of ice-cream.

Hot Cranberry Cider

1½ quarts cranberry juice	1.5 L
12 ounce orange juice cordial (concentrate)	350 ml
½ teaspoon cinnamon	2 ml

- Combine cranberry juice, orange juice cordial (concentrate) and 530 ml water in large saucepan. Bring to a boil to blend flavours.
- Add cinnamon and stir well.
- Serve hot.

Very Special Coffee Punch

I promise – this will make a hit!

2 ounce instant coffee	**55 g**
2¼ cups sugar	**540 ml**
2 quarts unthickened (half-and-half) cream	**2 L**
1 quart ginger ale	**1 L**
1 pint thickened (whipping) cream, whipped	**500 ml**
½ gallon French vanilla ice-cream	**2 L**

- Dissolve instant coffee in 2 L (2 quarts) hot water and cool. Add sugar and unthickened (half-and-half) cream, mix well and chill.
- When ready to serve, pour coffee-sugar mixture in punch bowl, add chilled ginger ale, whipped cream and ice-cream. Let some chunks of ice-cream remain.
- This will make 60 (120 ml/4 ounce) servings.

Mexican Coffee

1 ounce Kahlua®	**30 ml**
1 cup hot, black coffee	**240 ml**
Ground cinnamon	
Sweetened whipped cream	

- Pour Kahlua® and coffee into tall mug.
- Sprinkle with cinnamon and stir. Top with whipped cream.

Holiday Party Punch

The almond extract really gives this punch a special taste!

3 cups sugar	710 ml
6 ounce lemon gelatine	170 g
3 ounce orange juice cordial (concentrate)	90 ml
⅓ cup lemon juice	80 ml
46 ounce pineapple juice	1.35 L
3 tablespoons almond extract	45 ml
2 quarts ginger ale, chilled	2 L

- Combine sugar and 1 L (1 quart) water. Heat until sugar dissolves.
- Add gelatine and stir until it dissolves. Add cordial (concentrate), fruit juices, 1.5 L (1½ quarts) water and almond extract and chill.
- When ready to serve, place in punch bowl and add chilled ginger ale.
- This will make 50 servings.

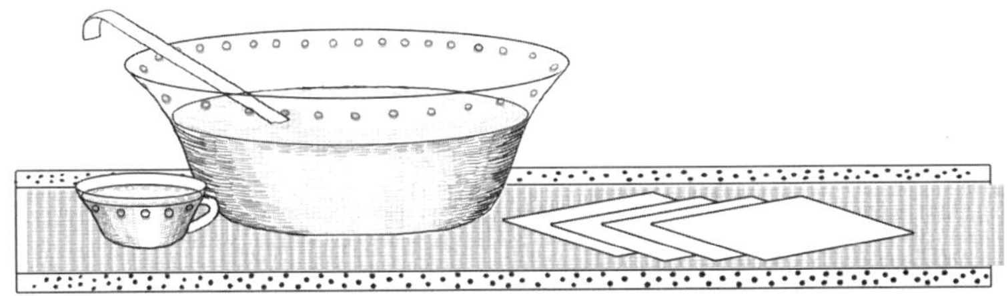

Green Party Punch

This punch would be great for St Patrick's Day!

3 ounce lime gelatine	85 g
6 ounce lime juice cordial (concentrate)	180 ml
6 ounce lemon juice cordial (concentrate)	180 ml
1 quart orange juice	1 L
1 quart pineapple juice	1 L
1 tablespoon almond extract	15 ml
2–3 drops green food colouring	
1 quart ginger ale, chilled	1 L

- Dissolve lime gelatine and 1 cup (240 ml) boiling water and stir well.
- In 4 L (1-gallon) bottle, combine dissolved gelatine, cordials (concentrates), orange juice, pineapple juice, almond essence and food colouring and chill.
- When ready to serve, add ginger ale.
- Serves 32.

Reception Punch

4 cups sugar	1 L
5 ripe bananas, mashed	
Juice of 2 lemons	
46 ounce pineapple juice	1.35 L
6 ounce orange juice cordial (concentrate)	180 ml
2 quarts ginger ale	2 L

- Boil sugar and 6 cups (1.5 L) water for 3 minutes and cool.
- Blend bananas with lemon juice and add pineapple juice and orange juice cordial (concentrate).
- Combine all ingredients except ginger ale. Freeze in large container.
- To serve, thaw 1½ hours, then add ginger ale. Punch will be slushy.
- Serves 40.

Strawberry Punch

20 ounce fresh strawberries, quartered	560 g
24 ounce raspberry cordial (concentrate)	710 ml
2 quart ginger ale, chilled	2 L

- Process strawberries through blender. Pour cordial (concentrate) into punch bowl and stir in strawberries.
- Add chilled ginger ale and stir well.

Sparkling Orange Punch

6 oranges, unpeeled, thinly sliced	
1 cup sugar	240 ml
2 bottles dry white wine	1.5 L
3 bottles sparkling wine, chilled	2.25 L

- Place orange slices in large plastic or glass container and sprinkle with sugar.
- Add white wine, cover and chill at least 8 hours.
- Stir in sparkling wine.

Strawberry Smoothie

2 medium bananas, peeled, sliced	
1 pint fresh strawberries, quartered	.5 kg
8 ounce strawberry yoghurt	225 g
¼ cup orange juice	60 ml

- Place all ingredients in blender. Process until smooth.
- Serve as is or over crushed ice.

Banana-Mango Smoothie

1 cup ripe mango, peeled, cubed	240 ml
1 ripe banana, sliced	
⅔ cup milk	160 ml
1 teaspoon honey	5 ml
¼ teaspoon vanilla extract	1 ml

- Arrange mango cubes in single layer on baking tray (sheet) and freeze about 1 hour or until firm.
- Combine frozen mango, banana, milk, honey and vanilla and pour into blender.
- Process until smooth.

BREAKFAST
& BRUNCH

Breakfast Bake

This is a favourite for overnight guests and even special enough for Christmas morning.

1 pound spicy sausage, cooked, crumbled	**.5 kg**
1 cup cheddar cheese, shredded	**240 ml**
1 cup scone (biscuit) mix	**240 ml**
5 eggs, slightly beaten	
2 cups milk	**240 ml**

- Preheat oven to 180° C (350° F).
- Place sausage in sprayed 23 x 33-cm (9 x 13-inch) baking dish and sprinkle with cheese.
- In mixing bowl, combine scone (biscuit) mix, eggs and a little salt and beat well.
- Add milk to egg mixture and stir until fairly smooth. Pour over sausage mixture.
- Bake for 35 minutes. (You can prepare this the night before cooking and refrigerate. To cook the next morning, add 5 minutes to cooking time.)

Breakfast Tacos

4 eggs	
4 flour tortillas	
1 cup cooked ham, chopped	240 ml
1 cup cheddar cheese, shredded	240 ml

- Scramble eggs in frying pan (skillet).
- Lay tortillas flat and spoon eggs over 4 tortillas.
- Sprinkle with ham and cheese and roll to enclose filling.
- Place tacos in microwave-safe dish and microwave for 30 seconds or until cheese melts.
- Serve immediately.

Bacon-Egg Burrito

2 slices bacon, cooked, chopped	
2 eggs, scrambled	
¼ cup cheddar cheese, shredded	60 ml
1 flour tortilla	
¼ cup salsa (optional)	60 ml

- Sprinkle bacon, eggs and cheese in middle of tortilla. (Add salsa if you like.)
- Fold tortilla sides over and place seam-side down on dinner plate.
- Microwave for 30 seconds or just until mixture heats thoroughly.

Glazed Bacon

1 pound bacon	.5 kg
⅓ cup brown sugar	80 ml
1 teaspoon plain (all-purpose) flour	5 ml
½ cup pecans, finely chopped	120 ml

- Preheat oven to 180° C (350° F).
- Arrange bacon slices close together, but not overlapping, on wire rack over drip pan.
- In bowl, combine brown sugar, flour and pecans and sprinkle evenly over bacon.
- Bake for 30 minutes. Drain on paper towels.

Curried Fruit Medley

29 ounce canned sliced peaches	820 g
2 (15 ounce) cans pineapple pieces (tidbits)	2 (425 g)
1 (10 ounce) jar glacé (maraschino) cherries	280 g
1 cup brown sugar	240 ml
1 teaspoon curry powder	5 ml
¼ cup butter, cut into pieces	60 ml

- Preheat oven to 180° C (350° F).
- Drain all fruit and place in 23 x 33-cm (9 x 13-inch) baking dish. Combine brown sugar and curry powder and stir well. Sprinkle over fruit and dot with butter.
- Bake covered for 30 minutes or until thoroughly hot.

Apricot Bake

4 (15 ounce) cans apricot halves, drained, divided	4 (425 g)
16 ounce light brown sugar, divided	.5 kg
2 cups round, buttery biscuit (cracker) crumbs, divided	480 ml
½ cup butter, sliced	120 ml

- Preheat oven to 150° C (300° F). Spray 23 x 33-cm (9 x 13-inch) baking dish and line with 2 cans drained apricots.
- Sprinkle half brown sugar and half biscuit (cracker) crumbs over apricots. Dot with half butter and repeat layers.
- Bake for 1 hour.

Pineapple-Cheese Casserole

This is really a different kind of recipe and very good. It can be served at brunch and is also great with sandwiches at lunch.

1 cup sugar	**240 ml**
5 tablespoons plain (all-purpose) flour	**75 ml**
2 (20 ounce) cans unsweetened pineapple pieces (tidbits), drained	**2 (565 g)**
1½ cups cheddar cheese, shredded	**360 ml**
1 tube round, buttery biscuits (crackers), crushed	
½ cup butter, melted	**120 ml**

- Preheat oven to 180° C (350° F).
- Combine sugar and flour.
- Spray 23 x 33-cm (9 x 13-inch) baking dish and layer pineapple, sugar-flour mixture, grated cheese and biscuit (cracker) crumbs (in that order).
- Drizzle butter over casserole.
- Bake for 25 minutes or until bubbly.

Ranch Sausage Bake

1 cup quick-cooking polenta (or grits)	240 ml
1 pound pork sausage meat	.5 kg
1 onion, chopped	
1 cup salsa	240 ml
8 ounce cheddar cheese, shredded, divided	225 g

- Preheat oven to 180° C (350° F).
- Cook polenta (or grits) according to package directions and set aside.
- Cook and brown sausage and onion and drain well.
- Combine polenta, sausage mixture, salsa and half of cheese and spoon into sprayed 2-L (2-quart) baking dish.
- Bake for 15 minutes.
- Remove from oven, add remaining cheese and bake additional 10 minutes.
- Serve hot.

This can also be a great dish for a Sunday night dinner.

Cinnamon Souffle

1 loaf cinnamon-raisin bread	
1 (20 ounce) can crushed pineapple with juice	565 g
1 cup butter, melted	240 ml
½ cup sugar	120 ml
5 eggs, lightly beaten	

- Preheat oven to 180° C (350° F).
- Slice very thin portion of bread crusts off.
- Tear bread into small pieces and place in sprayed 23 x 33-cm (9 x 13-inch) baking dish.
- Pour pineapple and juice over bread and set aside.
- Cream butter and sugar.
- Add eggs to creamed mixture and mix well.
- Pour creamed mixture over bread and pineapple. Bake uncovered for 40 minutes.

TIP: If you have some pecans handy, ½ cup chopped pecans adds extra texture and flavour.

Mexican Breakfast Eggs

¼ cup butter	**60 ml**
9 eggs	
3 tablespoons milk	**45 ml**
5 tablespoons salsa	**75 ml**
1 cup crushed corn (tortilla) chips	**240 ml**

- Melt butter in frying pan (skillet).
- In bowl, beat eggs and add milk and salsa.
- Pour egg mixture into pan and stir until eggs cook lightly.
- Stir in corn (tortilla) chips and serve hot.

Light, Crispy Waffles

2 cups scone (biscuit) mix	**480 ml**
1 egg	
½ cup oil	**120 ml**
1⅓ cups soda water (club soda)	**320 ml**

- Preheat waffle iron.
- Combine all ingredients in mixing bowl and stir by hand. Pour just enough batter to cover waffle iron and cook.

TIP: To have waffles for a 'company weekend', make them before the guests arrive. Freeze the waffles separately on a baking tray (sheet) and place in large plastic bags. To heat, bake at 175° C (350° F) for about 10 minutes.

Bacon-Sour Cream Omelette

2 eggs
5 strips bacon, fried, drained, crumbled, dripping retained
⅓ cup sour cream 80 ml
3 spring (green) onions, chopped
1 tablespoon butter 15 ml

- Use fork to beat eggs with 1 tablespoon (15 ml) water. Combine bacon and sour cream. Saute onions in bacon drippings and mix with bacon and sour cream.
- Melt butter in omelette pan. Pour in egg mixture and cook. When omelette is set, spoon sour cream mixture along centre and fold omelette onto warm plate.

Pineapple Coffee Cake

18 ounce butter cake mix 510 g
½ cup oil 120 ml
4 eggs, lightly beaten
1 (20 ounce) can crushed pineapple 565 g

- Preheat oven to 180° C (350° F). In mixing bowl combine cake mix, oil and eggs and beat well. Pour batter into sprayed, floured 23 x 33-cm (9 x 13-inch) baking pan.
- Bake for 45 to 50 minutes. Cake is done when toothpick inserted in centre comes out clean.
- Punch holes in cake about 5 cm (2 inches) apart with knife. Spread pineapple over cake while hot.

Cranberry Coffee Cake

2 eggs	
1 cup mayonnaise	240 ml
18 ounce cinnamon cake mix	510 g
2 teaspoons mixed spice	10 ml
16 ounce whole cranberry sauce	.5 kg
Icing (powdered) sugar	

- Preheat oven to 160° C (325° F).
- Beat together eggs, mayonnaise and cake mix with mixer and fold in cranberry sauce.
- Pour into sprayed, floured 23 x 33-cm (9 x 13-inch) baking pan.
- Bake for 45 minutes. Cake is done when toothpick inserted in centre comes out clean.
- When cake is cool, dust with icing (powdered) sugar. (If you would rather have icing than icing sugar, use prepared icing.)

Pecan Waffles

2 cups plain (all-purpose) flour	480 ml
½ cup oil	120 ml
½ cup milk	120 ml
⅔ cup pecans, finely chopped	160 ml

- Preheat waffle iron.
- In bowl, combine flour, oil and milk and mix well.
- Stir in chopped pecans.
- Pour approximately ¾ cup (180 ml) batter onto hot waffle iron and cook until brown and crispy.

Christmas Breakfast

12–14 eggs, lightly beaten	
1 pound sausage meat, cooked, drained, crumbled	.5 kg
2 cups milk	480 ml
1½ cups cheddar cheese, shredded	360 ml
5 ounce seasoned croutons	145 g

- Preheat oven to 180° C (350° F).
- Mix all ingredients and pour into 23 x 33-cm (9 x 13-inch) baking dish.
- Bake for 40 minutes.
- Let rest for about 10 minutes before serving.

Homemade Egg Substitute

6 egg whites	
¼ cup instant non-fat milk powder	60 ml
2 teaspoons oil	10 ml
¼ teaspoon ground turmeric	1 ml

- Combine all ingredients in blender, add 2 teaspoons (10 ml) water and process 30 seconds.
- Refrigerate.

Hot Green Squares

2 cups green chillies, chopped	480 ml
8 ounce sharp cheddar cheese, shredded	225 g
8 eggs, beaten	
½ cup unthickened (half-and-half) cream	120 ml

- Preheat oven to 180° C (350° F).
- Place green chillies in bottom of 23 x 33-cm (9 x 13-inch) baking pan and cover with cheese.
- Combine eggs, a little salt and pepper and cream and pour over chillies and cheese.
- Bake for 30 minutes.
- Let rest at room temperature for a few minutes before cutting into squares.

Baked Brunch

2 cups quick-cooking polenta (or grits)	480 ml
2 cups milk	480 ml
¾ cup butter	180 ml
4 eggs, beaten	

- Preheat oven to 180° C (350° F).
- Stir polenta (or grits) in 4 cups (1 L) water over medium heat for about 5 minutes.
- Add milk and butter, cover and cook additional 10 minutes.
- Remove from heat and add eggs.
- Pour in sprayed baking dish and bake for 30 minutes.

Praline Toast

½ cup butter, softened	120 ml
1 cup brown sugar	240 ml
½ cup pecans, finely chopped	120 ml
Bread slices	

- Combine butter, brown sugar and pecans and mix well.
- Spread butter mixture on bread slices.
- Toast in griller (broiler) until brown and bubbly.

Peach Bake

2 (15 ounce) cans peach halves, drained	2 (425 g)
1 cup brown sugar	240 ml
1 cup round, buttery biscuit (cracker) crumbs	240 ml
½ cup butter, melted	120 ml

- Preheat oven to 160° C (325° F).
- Spray 2-L (2-quart) baking dish and layer peaches, sugar and biscuit (cracker) crumbs until all ingredients are used. Pour melted butter over casserole.
- Bake for 35 minutes or until biscuit crumbs are slightly brown. Serve hot or at room temperature.

Sour Cream Rounds

2 cups plus 1 tablespoon plain (all-purpose) flour	480 ml/15 ml
3 teaspoons baking powder	15 ml
½ teaspoon bicarbonate of soda (baking soda)	2 ml
½ cup shortening	120 ml
8 ounce sour cream	225 g

- Preheat oven to 200° C (400° F). Combine dry ingredients, add a little salt and cut in shortening.
- Gradually add sour cream and mix lightly. Turn onto lightly floured board and knead a few times. Roll to 1.2-cm (½-inch) thickness. Cut with biscuit cutter and place on sprayed baking tray (sheet).
- Bake for 15 minutes or until light brown.

Cheesy Herb Bread

1 French stick (bread)	
½ teaspoon garlic powder	2 ml
1 teaspoon marjoram or oregano leaves	5 ml
1 tablespoon dried parsley leaves	15 ml
½ cup butter, softened	120 ml
1 cup parmesan cheese	240 ml

- Preheat oven to 190° C (375° F).
- Slice bread into 2.5-cm (1-inch) slices. Combine garlic, marjoram, parsley and butter. Spread mixture on bread slices and sprinkle with cheese.
- Wrap in foil and bake for 20 minutes. Unwrap and bake additional 5 minutes.

Garlic Toast

1 French stick (bread)	
1 tablespoon garlic powder	15 ml
2 tablespoons dried parsley flakes	30 ml
½ cup butter, melted	120 ml
1 cup parmesan cheese	240 ml

- Preheat oven to 110° C (225° F).
- Slice bread diagonally into 2.5-cm (1-inch) slices. Combine ingredients, except cheese, in small bowl and mix well. Brush mixture on bread and sprinkle cheese.
- Place on baking tray (sheet) and bake for about 1 hour.

Popovers

2 cups self-raising flour	480 ml
6 eggs, beaten	
2 cups milk	480 ml
Butter	

- Preheat oven to 220° C (425° F).
- Combine flour and 1 teaspoon (5 ml) salt in bowl. Add eggs and milk and mix. Add dry ingredients and mix well. (The batter will be like heavy cream.)
- Coat popover or muffin pans with butter and heat in oven. Fill each cup half full. Bake for 20 minutes. Reduce heat to 190° C (375° F) and bake additional 25 minutes. Serve immediately.

Easy Muffins

⅓ cup sugar	80 ml
⅓ cup oil	80 ml
¾ cup milk	180 ml
2 eggs	
2 cups scone (biscuit) mix	480 ml

- Preheat oven to 200° C (400° F).
- In mixing bowl, combine sugar, oil and milk. Beat in eggs and scone (biscuit) mix. Mix well; mixture will be a little lumpy. Pour into sprayed muffin pans two-thirds full.
- Bake for about 10 minutes or until light brown.

Spicy Cornbread Twists

3 tablespoons butter 45 ml
⅓ cup polenta (cornmeal) 80 ml
¼ teaspoon cayenne pepper 1 ml
11 ounce prepared bread dough, divided and shaped into 12 sticks 310 g

- Preheat oven to 180° C (350° F).
- Place butter in pie plate and melt in oven. Remove from oven.
- On wax paper, mix polenta (cornmeal) and cayenne pepper. Roll breadsticks in butter and cornmeal mixture.
- Twist breadsticks into a spiral shape and place on baking tray (sheet). Bake for 15 to 18 minutes.

Sausage Cornbread

1 (10 ounce) can creamed (cream-style) corn 280 g
2 eggs
¼ cup milk 60 ml
32 ounce prepared polenta (cornmeal) muffin mix 900 g
¼ pound pork sausage meat, cooked, drained, crumbled 110 g

- Preheat oven to 200° C (400° F).
- In bowl, combine corn, eggs and milk. Stir in muffin mix until just blended. Fold in sausage. Spoon mixture into sprayed 23 x 33-cm (9 x 13-inch) baking pan.
- Bake for about 20 minutes or until light brown.

Cream Rounds

2 cups plain (all-purpose) flour	480 ml
3 teaspoons baking powder	15 ml
8 ounce thickened (whipping) cream	225 g

- Preheat oven to 190° C (375° F).
- Combine flour, baking powder and ½ teaspoon (2 ml) salt. In mixing bowl, beat cream only until it holds a shape. Combine flour mixture and cream and mix with fork.
- Put dough on lightly floured board and knead about 1 minute. Pat dough to 1.8-cm (¾-inch) thickness. Cut out rounds with small biscuit (cookie) cutter.
- Bake on baking tray (sheet) for about 12 minutes or until light brown.

Orange French Toast

1 egg, beaten	
½ cup orange juice	120 ml
5 slices raisin bread	
1 cup crushed shredded wheatmeal biscuits (crackers)	240 ml
2 tablespoons butter	30 ml

- Combine egg and orange juice. Dip bread in mixture and then in crumbs.
- Fry in butter until brown.

Strawberry Bread

Great for finger food at parties or as sandwiches with cream cheese and pecans, and red is always 'in'!

3 cups self-raising flour	**720 ml**
1 teaspoon bicarbonate of soda (baking soda)	**5 ml**
1 teaspoon cinnamon	**5 ml**
2 cups sugar	**480 ml**
20 ounce strawberries, quartered	**560 g**
1¼ cups oil	**300 ml**
4 eggs, beaten	
1 teaspoon red food colouring	**5 ml**

- Preheat oven to 180° C (350° F).
- Combine flour, bicarbonate of soda (baking soda), cinnamon, ½ teaspoon (2 ml) salt and sugar in mixing bowl.
- With spoon, make a well in dry ingredients, add strawberries, oil and eggs and mix well. Add food colouring and mix well.
- Pour into 2 sprayed, floured loaf pans.
- Bake for 1 hour.

You can save some time by slicing or chopping vegetables all at one time, then storing them in plastic bags in the refrigerator. When you're ready to use them, just pull out the bag and use what you need. You'll be surprised how nice it is.

Caramel Rolls

9 tablespoons butter, softened, divided	115 ml
1 cup light brown sugar	240 ml
½ cup pecans, chopped	120 ml
16 ounce prepared bread mix (dough)	450 g
¼ cup sugar	60 ml
2 teaspoons cinnamon	10 ml

- Preheat oven to 190° C (375° F).
- In unsprayed 23 x 33-cm (9 x 13-inch) pan, melt 5 tablespoons (75 ml) butter in oven. Stir in brown sugar, ¼ cup (60 ml) water and pecans and set aside.
- Separate dough into 8 rectangles.
- Spread with 4 tablespoons (60 ml) softened butter. Combine sugar and cinnamon and sprinkle over dough.
- Starting at shorter side, roll each rectangle and cut each roll into 4 slices, making 32 pieces. Place in prepared pan.
- Bake for 20 to 25 minutes or until golden brown. Invert immediately to remove from pan and serve warm.

Apricot-Pineapple Muffins

⅓ cup dried apricots, very finely cut	80 ml
½ cup butter, softened	120 ml
1 cup sugar	240 ml
1 egg	
1 (8 ounce) can crushed pineapple with juice	225 g
1¼ cups flour	300 ml
½ teaspoon bicarbonate of soda (baking soda)	2 ml
1 cup quick-rolled oats	240 ml

- Preheat oven to 180° C (350° F). With mixer, cream butter and sugar, add egg and pineapple and beat well. Add all dry ingredients and ½ teaspoon (2 ml) salt, mix well and fold in apricots.
- Spoon into well sprayed muffin cups or use the paper liners. Bake for 20 minutes. Makes 12 muffins.

French Onion Drops

2 cups scone (biscuit) mix	480 ml
¼ cup milk	60 ml
1 (8 ounce) container French onion dip	225 g
2 tablespoons spring (green) onion, finely minced	30 ml

- Preheat oven to 200° C (400° F).
- Mix all ingredients until soft dough forms.
- Drop by teaspoonfuls onto sprayed baking tray (sheet). Bake for 10 minutes or until light brown.

Eagle Yeast Bread

8 cups sifted plain (all-purpose) flour, divided	**1.9 L**
1 tablespoon sugar	**15 ml**
2 tablespoons baking yeast (2 yeast cakes)	
1 (14 ounce) can sweetened condensed milk	**415 ml**
⅓ cup oil	**80 ml**

- Combine 6 cups flour, sugar and 1 tablespoon (15 ml) salt and set aside.
- Soften yeast in small amount of warm water. Add sweetened condensed milk, oil and enough warm water to measure 4 cups (1 L) and mix well.
- Add to flour mixture and mix well. Add remaining 2 cups (480 ml) flour and mix well.
- Knead 10 minutes. Place in sprayed bowl and turn out onto sprayed surface.
- Let rise, covered, for 1½ to 2 hours or until doubled in size.
- Divide into 3 portions. Place in 3 sprayed loaf pans. Let rise 40 minutes.
- Preheat oven to 180° C (350° F).
- Bake approximately 40 minutes. Brush with melted butter.

Cheese Drops

2 cups scone (biscuit) mix	**480 ml**
⅔ cup milk	**160 ml**
⅔ cup sharp cheddar cheese, shredded	**160 ml**
¼ cup butter, melted	**60 ml**

- Preheat oven to 200° C (400° F).
- Combine scone (biscuit) mix, milk and cheese. Drop 1 heaping tablespoon (15 ml) dough onto sprayed baking tray (sheet) for each scone. Bake for 10 minutes or until light brown.
- While warm, brush tops of scone with melted butter. Serve hot.

Bacon-Cheese French Bread

1 (16 ounce) unsliced French stick (bread)	**.5 kg**
5 slices bacon, cooked, crumbled	
8 ounce mozzarella cheese, shredded	**225 g**
½ cup butter, melted	**120 ml**

- Preheat oven to 180° C (350° F).
- Slice bread into 2.5-cm (1-inch) slices and place sliced stick on large piece of aluminium foil.
- Combine bacon and cheese and sprinkle between slices of bread. Drizzle butter over stick and let some drip in between slices.
- Wrap stick tightly in foil. Bake for 20 minutes or until thoroughly hot. Serve hot.

Crunchy Breadsticks

8 hot dog buns	
1 cup butter, melted	240 ml
2 cloves garlic, crushed	
Paprika	

- Preheat oven to 110° C (225° F).
- Take each half bun and slice in half lengthwise.
- Mix the garlic and butter together. Use pastry brush to butter all breadsticks. Sprinkle each breadstick lightly with paprika. Place on baking tray (sheet) and bake for 45 minutes.

Maple Syrup Rounds

2¼ cups scone (biscuit) mix	540 ml
⅔ cup milk	160 ml
1½ cups maple syrup	360 ml

- Preheat oven to 220° C (425° F). Combine scone (biscuit) mix and milk and stir until moist. On floured surface, roll dough to 1.2-cm (½-inch) thickness. Cut out rounds with 5-cm (2-inch) biscuit (cookie) cutter.
- Pour syrup into 18 x 28-cm (7 x 11-inch) baking dish. Place rounds on top of syrup. Bake for 13 to 15 minutes or until golden brown.

Mozzarella Loaf

1 (16 ounce) unsliced French stick	.5 kg
12 slices mozzarella cheese	
¼ cup parmesan cheese, grated	60 ml
6 tablespoons butter, softened	90 ml
½ teaspoon garlic salt	2 ml

- Preheat oven to 190° C (375° F).
- Cut loaf into 2.5-cm (1-inch) thick slices. Place mozzarella slices between bread slices. Combine parmesan cheese, butter and garlic salt and spread on bread slices.
- Reshape loaf, press together and brush remaining butter mixture on outside of loaf. Bake 8 to 10 minutes.

Cheddar Cornbread

17 ounce prepared polenta (cornmeal)	480 g
2 eggs, beaten	
½ cup milk	120 ml
½ cup plain yoghurt	120 ml
1 (14 ounce) can creamed (cream-style) corn	395 g
½ cup cheddar cheese, shredded	120 ml

- Preheat oven to 200° C (400° F).
- In bowl, combine muffin mix, eggs, milk and yoghurt until they blend. Stir in corn and cheese and pour into sprayed 23 x 33-cm (9 x 13-inch) baking dish.
- Bake for 18 to 20 minutes or until light brown.

Raspberry-Filled Blueberry Muffins

1(16 ounce) box blueberry muffin mix with blueberries	.5 kg
1 egg	
⅓ cup red raspberry jam	80 ml
¼ cup sliced almonds	60 ml

- Preheat oven to 190° C (375° F).
- Rinse blueberries and drain.
- In bowl, combine muffin mix, egg and ½ cup (120 ml) water. Stir until moist and break up any lumps in mix.
- Place paper liners in 8 muffin cups. Fill cups half full with batter. Combine raspberry jam with blueberries and spoon mixture over batter.
- Cover with remaining batter and sprinkle almonds over batter. Bake for 18 minutes or until light brown.

Ham-Cheese Bars

2 cups scone (biscuit) mix	480 ml
1 heaped cup cooked, finely chopped ham	240 ml
1 cup cheddar cheese, shredded	240 ml
½ onion, finely chopped	
½ cup parmesan cheese, grated	120 ml
¼ cup sour cream	60 ml
1 clove garlic, crushed	5 ml
1 cup milk	240 ml
1 egg	

- Preheat oven to 180° C (350° F).
- Combine all ingredients plus ½ teaspoon (2 ml) salt in mixing bowl and mix by hand.
- Spread in sprayed 23 x 33-cm (9 x 13-inch) baking pan. Bake for 30 minutes or until light brown.
- Cut in rectangles, about 2 x 2.5-cm (2 x 1-inch). Serve hot or at room temperature.

TIP: These bars go well with a lot of our brunch casseroles. They can be served at brunch or lunch and they can be kept in the refrigerator (cooked) and reheated. To reheat, place in a 160° C (325° F) oven for about 15 minutes. They will be good and crispy when reheated.

SOUPS
& SALADS

Broccoli-Wild Rice Soup

This is a hardy and delicious soup that is full of flavour.

1 (6 ounce) package chicken-flavoured wild rice mix — 170 g
10 ounce broccoli, chopped — 280 g
2 teaspoons dried minced onion — 10 ml
1 (10 ounce) can cream of chicken soup — 280 g
8 ounce cream cheese, cubed — 225 g

- In large saucepan, combine rice, rice seasoning and 6 cups (1.5 L) water.
- Boil, reduce heat, cover and simmer for 10 minutes, stir once. Stir in broccoli and onion and simmer 5 minutes.
- Stir in soup and cream cheese. Cook and stir until cheese melts.

Ham and Bean Soup

3 (16 ounce) cans cannellini (navy) beans with liquid — 3 (.5 kg)
1 (14 ounce) can chicken liquid stock (broth) — 415 ml
1 cup ham, chopped — 240 ml
1 large onion, chopped
1 clove garlic, crushed — 2 ml

- In large saucepan, combine all ingredients, add 1 cup (240 ml) water and bring to a boil.
- Simmer until onion is tender and serve hot with cornbread.

Creamy Veggie Soup

1 pound fresh zucchini (courgettes), grated	**.5 kg**
1 onion, chopped	
1 (14 ounce) can chicken liquid stock (broth)	**415 ml**
½ teaspoon sweet basil	**2 ml**
2 cups unthickened (half-and-half) cream, divided	**480 ml**

- In saucepan, combine zucchini (courgettes), onion, stock, basil and a little salt and pepper.
- Bring to a boil, simmer until soft, pour into food processor and puree.
- Gradually add ½ cup (120 ml) cream and blend. (You could add ¼ teaspoon/1 ml curry powder, if you like curry flavour.)
- Return zucchini mixture to saucepan and add remaining cream. Heat but do not boil.

Tomato-French Onion Soup

1 (10 ounce) can cream of tomato soup	**280 g**
2 (10 ounce) cans French onion soup	**2 (280 g)**
Parmesan cheese, grated	
Croutons	

- In saucepan, combine soups with 2 soup cans water and heat thoroughly.
- To serve, pour soup into individual bowls and top with croutons and cheese.

Easy Potato Soup

1 (16 ounce) package hash browns, shredded	.5 kg
1 cup onion, chopped	240 ml
14 ounce chicken liquid stock (broth)	415 ml
1 (10 ounce) can cream of celery soup	280 g
1 (10 ounce) can cream of chicken soup	280 g
2 cups milk	480 ml

- In large saucepan, combine hash browns, onion and 2 cups (480 ml) water and bring to a boil. Cover, reduce heat and simmer 30 minutes.
- Stir in stock (broth), soups and milk and heat thoroughly. (If you like, garnish with shredded cheddar cheese or cooked, diced ham.)

Fast Fiesta Soup

1 (15 ounce) can tomatoes with chopped fresh coriander (cilantro) and lime juice added (to taste)	425 g
1 (15 ounce) can corn kernels (sweetcorn)	425 g
1 (15 ounce) can borlotti (pinto) beans with liquid	425 g
28 ounce chicken liquid stock (broth)	830 ml
1 (10 ounce) jar processed cream cheese with chopped jalapeño chillies	280 g
12 ounce chicken breast, cooked, diced	340 g

- Brown chicken in frying pan (skillet) on low heat for 3–5 minutes
- Combine tomatoes, corn, beans, stock (broth) and cream cheese in large soup pot, heat 10 minutes and mix well. Stir in chicken until thoroughly hot.

Southwestern Soup

1½ pounds lean beef mince	.7 kg
1 large onion, chopped	
3 (15 ounce) cans borlotti (pinto) beans with liquid	3 (425 g)
2 (15 ounce) cans corn kernels (sweetcorn) with liquid	2 (425 g)
2 (15 ounce) cans tomatoes with chopped fresh coriander (cilantro) and lime juice added (to taste)	2 (425 g)
2 (1 ounce) packets taco seasoning	2 (30 g)

- Brown beef and onion in large soup pot, stir until beef crumbles and drain. Add beans, corn, tomatoes and 1½ cups (360 ml) water. Boil, reduce heat and stir in taco seasoning. Simmer for 25 minutes.

Speedy Vegetable Soup

1 pound lean beef mince	.5 kg
2 (15 ounce) cans stewed tomatoes	2 (425 g)
42 ounce beef liquid stock (broth)	1.25 L
1 (16 ounce) package frozen mixed vegetables	.5 kg
½ cup instant brown rice	120 ml

- Brown beef in frying pan (skillet) and stir until beef crumbles. Transfer to soup pot and add tomatoes, beef stock (broth) and vegetables. Boil, reduce heat and simmer for 20 minutes and stir occasionally. Add brown rice and cook on medium heat for 5 minutes.

Chicken-Broccoli Soup

28 ounce chicken liquid stock (broth)	830 ml
1 bunch spring (green) onions, finely chopped, divided	
10 ounce broccoli, chopped	280 g
1½ cups mashed potato	360 ml
2½ cups cooked, cut-up chicken breasts	600 ml
8 ounce mozzarella cheese, shredded	225 g
8 ounce thickened (whipping) cream	240 ml
1 cup milk	240 ml

- Combine stock (broth), half spring (green) onions and broccoli in large saucepan. Boil, reduce heat, cover and simmer for 5 minutes.
- Stir in mashed potato and mix until blended. Add chicken, cheese, cream, milk, 1 cup (240 ml) water and a little salt and pepper. Heat over medium heat and stir occasionally until hot and cheese melts, about 5 minutes.
- Ladle into individual soup bowls and garnish with remaining chopped spring onions.

Creamy Turkey Soup

42 ounce chicken liquid stock (broth)	1.25 L
1 pound potatoes, peeled, cubed	.5 kg
3 sticks celery, sliced	
1 (15 ounce) can carrots, sliced, drained	425 g
10 ounce yellow squash, chopped	280 g
2 cloves garlic, crushed	10 ml
1 teaspoon dried thyme	5 ml
1½ cups shredded turkey	360 ml
1 (10 ounce) can cream of chicken soup	280 g
1 cup milk or unthickened (half-and-half) cream	240 ml

- Combine chicken stock (broth), ½ cup (120 ml) water, potatoes and celery in soup pot and boil. Add a little salt and pepper and cook on medium heat about 20 minutes or until potatoes and celery are tender. Add carrots, squash, garlic and thyme and cook another 10 minutes.
- Stir in shredded turkey, chicken soup and milk and heat just until soup is thoroughly hot, but do not boil.

Spicy Beef Soup

1 pound lean beef mince (ground beef)	.5 kg
8 ounce onions, chopped	250 g
8 ounce capsicum (pepper), chopped	250 g
2 tablespoons oil	30 ml
1 (10 ounce) package frozen corn	280 g
28 ounce beef liquid stock (broth)	830 ml
1 (15 ounce) can borlotti (pinto) beans with liquid	425 g
2 tablespoons chilli powder	30 ml
1 teaspoon ground cumin	5 ml

- In large frying pan (skillet), brown beef, onions and capsicum (pepper) in oil.
- Transfer to soup pot and add corn, stock (broth), beans, chilli powder, cumin and a little salt and pepper.
- Boil, reduce heat and simmer for 30 minutes. Serve hot.

TIP: For a spicier soup, you could add 1 (280 g/10 ounce) can tomatoes and chopped green chillies to taste.

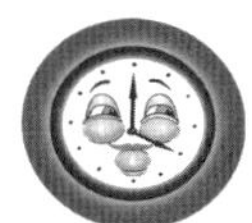

Meatball Soup

1 (18 ounce) package frozen, cooked Italian meatballs	510 g
28 ounce beef liquid stock (broth)	830 ml
2 (15 ounce) cans Italian stewed tomatoes	2 (425 g)
1 (16 ounce) package frozen mixed vegetables	.5 kg

- Place meatballs, beef stock (broth) and tomatoes in large saucepan. Boil, reduce heat and simmer 10 minutes or until meatballs are thoroughly hot. Add vegetables and cook on medium heat for 10 minutes.

TIP: For thicker soup, mix 2 tablespoons (30 ml) cornflour (cornstarch) in ¼ cup (60 ml) water. Add to soup, boil and stir until soup thickens.

Potato-Sausage Soup

1 pound pork sausages	.5 kg
1 cup celery, chopped	240 ml
1 cup onion, chopped	240 ml
2 (10 ounce) cans potato soup	2 (280 g)
14 ounce chicken liquid stock (broth)	415 ml

- Cut sausage into 2.5-cm (1-inch) diagonal slices. Brown sausage in large heavy soup pot, drain and place in separate bowl. Leave about 2 tablespoons (30 ml) sausage drippings in pot and saute celery and onion.
- Add potato soup, ¾ cup (180 ml) water, chicken stock (broth) and sausage. Boil, reduce heat and simmer for 20 minutes.

Winter Stew

This is a great choice for a cold, winter day.

1½ pounds lean beef mince (ground beef)	.7 kg
1 onion, chopped	
1 (1 ounce) packet taco seasoning	30 g
1 (1 ounce) packet French onion soup mix	30 g
1 (15 ounce) can corn kernels (sweetcorn), drained	425 g
1 (15 ounce) can kidney beans with liquid	425 g
2 (15 ounce) cans borlotti (pinto) beans	2 (425 g)
2 (15 ounce) cans tomatoes with chopped fresh coriander (cilantro) and lime juice added (to taste)	2 (425 g)
1 (10 ounce) can tomatoes	280 g
2 ounce jar chopped green chillies	40 g

- Brown beef and onion in large sauce pan. Add soup and seasoning and mix well.
- Add corn, beans, tomatoes and green chillies and 1 cup (240 ml) water, mix well and simmer for about 30 minutes.

Beefy Bean Chilli

2 pounds lean beef mince (ground beef)	1 kg
3 sticks celery, sliced	
1 onion, chopped	
1 capsicum (pepper), seeded, chopped	
2 cloves garlic, crushed	10 ml
1 (15 ounce) jar tomato pasta sauce	425 g
3 tablespoons chilli powder	45 ml
2 (15 ounce) cans borlotti (pinto) beans with liquid	2 (425 g)
1–2 cups crushed corn (tortilla) chips	240 ml

- Brown beef in large soup pot over medium heat until meat crumbles. Add celery, onion, capsicum (bell pepper) and minced garlic. Cook for 5 minutes or until vegetables are tender, but not brown.
- Stir in tomato pasta sauce, chilli powder, 2 cups (480 ml) water and a little salt and pepper and mix well. Bring mixture to a boil, reduce heat and simmer for 35 minutes.
- Add beans during last 15 minutes of cooking time. Ladle into individual serving bowls and top each serving with several tablespoons crushed chips.

Hearty Bean and Ham Soup

What a great supper for a cold winter night!

¼ cup butter	60 ml
15 ounce carrots, sliced	425 g
1 cup celery, chopped	240 ml
1 cup green capsicum (pepper), chopped	240 ml
2–3 cups cooked, diced ham	480 ml
2 (15 ounce) cans cannellini (navy) beans with liquid	2 (425 g)
2 (15 ounce) cans borlotti (pinto) beans with liquid and chopped jalapeño chillies	2 (425 g)
28 ounce chicken liquid stock (broth)	830 ml
2 teaspoons chilli powder	10 ml

- Cook carrots, celery and capsicum (pepper) in soup pot with butter about 8 minutes until tender but crisp.
- Add diced ham, beans, jalapeños, chicken stock (broth), chilli powder and a little salt and pepper. Boil and stir constantly for 3 minutes. Reduce heat and simmer for 15 minutes.

TIP: Cornbread is great with this soup and it's so quick and easy to make.

Soup with an Attitude

1 (32 ounce) carton chicken liquid stock (broth)	1 L
3 large potatoes, peeled, grated	
2 onions, finely chopped	
3 sticks celery, sliced	
8 ounce peas	225 g
7 ounce green chillies, chopped	200 g
3 cups ham, chopped	710 ml
16 ounce processed cheese, cubed	.5 kg
1 pint unthickened (half-and-half) cream	500 ml

- Combine stock (broth), potatoes, onions, celery, peas, chillies and ham in soup pot. Stirring, bring to a boil, reduce heat to medium-low and simmer 30 minutes.
- On medium heat, add cheese and stir constantly until cheese melts. Stir in cream and continue cooking until soup is thoroughly hot; do not boil.

Cabbage-Ham Soup

1 (16 ounce) package shredded cabbage (cabbage slaw)	.5 kg
1 onion, chopped	
1 red capsicum (pepper), seeded, chopped	
1 clove garlic, crushed	5 ml
28 ounce chicken liquid stock (broth)	830 ml
1 (15 ounce) can stewed tomatoes	425 g
2 cups cooked, cubed ham	480 ml
¼ cup brown sugar	60 ml
2 tablespoons lemon juice	30 ml

- Combine shredded cabbage (cabbage slaw), onion, capsicum (pepper), garlic, chicken stock (broth) and 1 cup water in large, heavy soup pot. Boil, reduce heat and simmer for 20 minutes.
- Stir in tomatoes, ham, 1 teaspoon (5 ml) salt, brown sugar, lemon juice and a little pepper. Heat just until soup is thoroughly hot.

Ham and Corn Soup

3 medium potatoes, cubed	
28 ounce chicken liquid stock (broth), divided	830 ml
2 sticks celery, chopped	
1 onion, chopped	
4 tablespoons plain (all-purpose) flour	60 ml
1 pint unthickened (half-and-half) cream	500 ml
½ teaspoon cayenne pepper	2 ml
1 (15 ounce) can corn kernels (sweetcorn)	425 g
1 (15 ounce) can creamed (cream-style) corn	425 g
3 cups cooked, cubed ham	710 ml
8 ounce processed cheese, grated	227 g

- Cook potatoes with 415 ml (14 ounce) chicken stock (broth) in saucepan. Saute celery and onion in large soup pot with a little oil.
- On medium heat add flour and mix well. Add remaining stock and cream. Cook, stirring constantly, until mixture thickens.
- Add potatoes, cayenne pepper, corn, ham, cheese and a little salt and pepper. Heat slowly and stir several times to keep from sticking.

When you're pouring soup or stew from one container to another, pour it over the back of a large spoon. The spoon will reduce the splatter and the process will be neater with less clean-up.

Rich Corn Soup

8 ears fresh corn	
8 slices bacon	
1 small onion, chopped	
½ red capsicum (pepper), seeded, chopped	
1 small baking potato, peeled, cubed	
1 pint unthickened (half-and-half) cream	500 ml
2 teaspoons sugar	10 ml
½ teaspoon dried thyme	2 ml
1 tablespoon cornflour (cornstarch)	15 ml

- Cut corn from cobs into large bowl and scrape well to remove all milk.
- Fry bacon in large soup pot over medium heat, remove bacon and save drippings in pan. Crumble bacon and set aside.
- Cook onion and capsicum (pepper) in drippings until tender. Stir in corn, potato, 1 cup (240 ml) water and a little salt and pepper. Boil, cover, reduce heat and simmer for 15 minutes, stirring occasionally.
- Stir in 1½ cups (360 ml) cream, sugar and thyme. Combine cornflour (cornstarch) and remaining cream and stir until smooth. Gradually add to corn mixture and stir constantly.
- Cook uncovered for 15 minutes, stirring constantly, until soup thickens.

Sausage-Vegetable Soup

1 pound Italian sausage	.5 kg
2 onions, chopped	
2 cloves garlic, crushed	10 ml
1 (1 ounce) packet beef soup mix	30 ml
15 ounce carrots, sliced	425 g
2 (15 ounce) cans Italian stewed tomatoes	2 (425 g)
2 (15 ounce) cans chickpeas (garbanzo beans), drained	2 (425 g)
1 cup elbow macaroni	240 ml

- Brown sausage, onions and garlic in large soup pot. Drain and add 4 cups (1 L) water, soup mix, carrots, tomatoes and chickpeas (garbanzo beans). Boil, reduce heat and simmer for 25 minutes.
- Add elbow macaroni and continue cooking additional 15 to 20 minutes or until macaroni is tender.

Seafood Bisque

¼ cup butter	60 ml
8 ounce salad shrimp	225 g
1 (6 ounce) can crabmeat, drained, flaked	170 g
15 ounce whole new potatoes	425 g
1 clove garlic, crushed	5 ml
½ cup plain (all-purpose) flour	120 ml
28 ounce chicken liquid stock (broth), divided	830 ml
1 cup unthickened (half-and-half) cream	240 ml

- Melt butter and cook on medium heat in large saucepan. Add shrimp, crabmeat, new potatoes and garlic and cook for 10 minutes.
- Stir in flour and cook, stirring constantly, for 3 minutes. Gradually add chicken stock (broth), cook and stir until mixture thickens.
- Stir in cream and a little salt and pepper, stirring constantly and cook just until mixture is thoroughly hot; do not boil.

The best way to keep cleaned fish from getting freezer burn is to fill a plastic bag about half full of water. Add fish and add more water so fish is covered. Seal and record the date the fish is frozen.

Fresh Oyster Stew

2 pints fresh oysters with liquid	1 kg
3 slices bacon	
1 small onion, chopped	
2 sticks celery, chopped	
1 (4 ounce) can sliced mushrooms	115 g
1 (10 ounce) can cream of potato soup	280 g
3 cups unthickned (half-and-half) cream	710 ml
⅓ cup fresh parsley, chopped	80 ml

- Drain oysters and save liquid. Fry bacon until crisp, drain bacon and crumble. Set aside.
- On medium heat in large frying pan (skillet), cook onion and celery in bacon fat until tender.
- Add mushrooms, soup, oyster liquid, cream and a little salt and pepper. Heat over medium heat, stirring occasionally, until mixture is thoroughly hot.
- Stir in bacon and oysters and heat 4 to 5 minutes longer or until edges of oysters begin to curl. Sprinkle with parsley.

A real time-saver is to make a large pot of soup or stew and freeze it in portions in large plastic bags. Freeze enough for one, two or four. When the bag is sealed, it will lay flat in the freezer and won't take up as much room as containers. Be sure to leave a little room for expansion as it freezes.

Incredible Broccoli-Cheese Soup

This really is an incredible soup!

10 ounce broccoli, chopped	**280 g**
3 tablespoons butter	**45 ml**
¼ onion, finely chopped	
¼ cup plain (all-purpose) flour	**60 ml**
1 pint unthickened (half-and-half) cream	**500 ml**
14 ounce chicken liquid stock (broth)	**415 ml**
⅛ teaspoon cayenne pepper	**.5 ml**
8 ounce processed cheese, cubed	**115 g**

- Cook broccoli in steamer until tender.
- Melt butter and saute onion in large saucepan, but do not brown. Add flour, stir and gradually add cream, chicken stock (broth), ½ teaspoon (2 ml) salt, ⅛ teaspoon (.5 ml) pepper and cayenne pepper. Stir constantly and heat until mixture is slightly thick. Do not let mixture boil!
- Add cheese, stir constantly and heat until cheese melts. Add cooked broccoli. Serve piping hot.

Bean Soup

Don't let the number of ingredients discourage you. Ask yourself this question, 'Can I open cans?'

¼ cup butter	60 ml
1 onion, chopped	
1 capsicum (pepper), seeded, chopped	
2 teaspoons minced garlic	10 ml
2 (15 ounce) cans tomatoes with chopped fresh coriander (cilantro) and lime juice added (to taste)	2 (425 g)
1 (15 ounce) can borlotti (pinto) beans, drained	425 g
1 (15 ounce) can kidney beans, rinsed, drained	425 g
1 (15 ounce) can black beans, rinsed, drained	425 g
1 tablespoon chilli powder	15 ml
¼ teaspoon ground coriander	1 ml
1 cup shredded cheddar with finely chopped jalapeños (Mexicana cheese)	240 ml
1 cup shredded cheddar cheese, divided	240 ml

- Melt butter in large saucepan on medium heat and cook onion, capsicum (pepper) and garlic for 5 minutes. Stir in tomatoes, all 3 cans beans, chilli powder, coriander and a little salt and pepper.
- Boil, reduce heat, cover and simmer for 25 minutes.
- Stir in cheese and jalapeños and cook over low heat, stirring occasionally, just until cheese melts.
- Ladle into individual soup bowls and sprinkle cheddar cheese over each serving.

Italian Minestrone

1 cup onions, chopped	240 ml
1 cup capsicum (peppers), chopped	240 ml
3 sticks celery, chopped	
2 teaspoons minced garlic	10 ml
¼ cup butter	60 ml
2 (15 ounce) cans diced tomatoes	2 (425 g)
1 teaspoon dried oregano	5 ml
1 teaspoon dried basil	5 ml
28 ounce beef liquid stock (broth)	830 ml
2 (15 ounce) cans cannellini (navy) beans	2 (425 g)
2 medium zucchini (courgettes), cut in half lengthwise, sliced	
1 cup elbow macaroni	240 ml

- Saute onions, capsicum (peppers), celery and garlic in butter for about 2 minutes in soup pot. Add tomatoes, oregano, basil and a little salt and pepper. Boil, reduce heat and simmer for 15 minutes, stirring occasionally.
- Stir in beef stock (broth), beans, zucchini (courgettes) and macaroni and boil. Reduce heat and simmer another 15 minutes or until macaroni is tender.

Broccoli-Noodle Salad

1 cup slivered almonds, toasted	240 ml
1 cup sunflower seeds, toasted	240 ml
2 (3 ounce) packages chicken-flavoured ramen noodles	2 (85 g)
16 ounce broccoli, finely chopped	.5 kg
1 (8 ounce) bottle Italian salad dressing	240 ml

- Toast almonds and sunflower seeds in oven at 135° C (275° F) for about 10 minutes.
- Break up ramen noodles and mix with broccoli, almonds and sunflower seeds. Toss with Italian salad dressing and chill.

Winter Salad

1 (15 ounce) can cut green beans, drained	425 g
1 (15 ounce) can green peas, drained	425 g
1 (15 ounce) can corn kernels (sweetcorn), drained	425 g
1 (15 ounce) can kidney beans, drained	425 g
1 (2 ounce) jar green chillies	55 g
1 (8 ounce) bottle Italian salad dressing	240 ml

- Combine all vegetables in large bowl.
- Pour Italian dressing over vegetables. Cover and refrigerate.

Nutty Green Salad

6 cups mixed salad greens, torn	1.5 L
1 medium zucchini (courgette), sliced	
1 (8 ounce) can sliced water chestnuts, drained	225 g
½ cup peanuts	120 ml
⅓ cup Italian salad dressing	80 ml

- Toss greens, zucchini (courgette), water chestnuts and peanuts.
- When ready to serve, add salad dressing and toss.

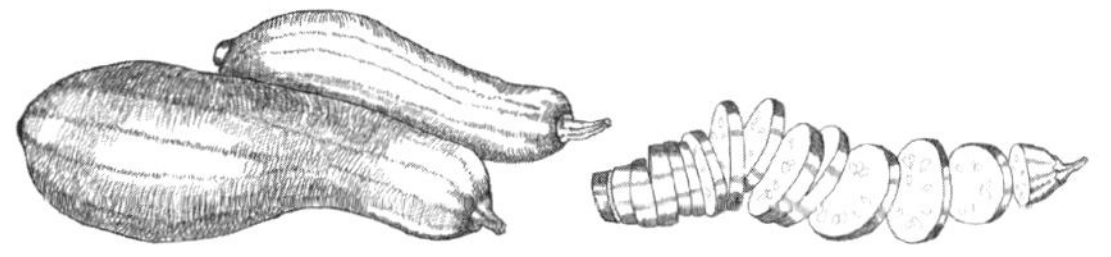

Green and Red Salad

4 cups mixed salad greens, torn	1 L
3 spring (green) onions with tops, chopped	
2 medium red apples, diced	
1 cup fresh raspberries	240 ml
½ cup poppy seed dressing	120 ml

- In bowl, toss salad greens, onions and fruit.
- Drizzle with dressing and toss.

Special Rice Salad

1 (6 ounce) package chicken-flavoured rice	170 g
¾ cup green capsicum (pepper), chopped	180 ml
1 bunch spring (green) onion with tops, chopped	
2 (6 ounce) jars marinated artichoke hearts	2 (170 g)
½–⅔ cup mayonnaise	120 ml

- Cook rice and macaroni according to directions (but with no butter), drain and cool.
- Add green capsicum (pepper), onions, artichoke hearts and mayonnaise, toss and chill.

Chicken Salad

3 cups boneless, skinless chicken breast halves, cooked, chopped	710 ml
1½ cups celery, chopped	360 ml
½ cup sweet pickle relish	120 ml
2 eggs, hard-boiled, chopped	
¾ cup mayonnaise	180 ml

- Combine all ingredients and several sprinkles salt and pepper.

Fantastic Fruit Salad

22 ounce mandarine pieces (tidbits)	620 g
2 (15 ounce) cans pineapple pieces (tidbits)	2 (425 g)
16 ounce fresh strawberries, halved	.5 kg
1 (20 ounce) can peach slices	565 g
1 (20 ounce) can apricot halves	565 g

- Drain mandarine and pineapple.
- Combine all ingredients and fold together gently.

Peachy Fruit Salad

2 (20 ounce) cans sliced peaches	2 (565 g)
1 (20 ounce) can pineapple pieces (tidbits), drained	565 g
11 ounce mandarine pieces (tidbits)	310 g
1 (8 ounce) jar glacé (maraschino) cherries, drained	225 g
1 cup miniature marshmallows	240 ml

- Combine all ingredients in large bowl, fold together gently and refrigerate.
- Serve in pretty crystal bowl. (Bananas may be added if you like.)

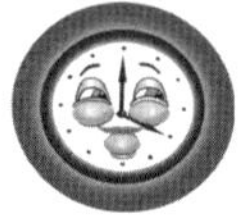

Cherry Salad

1 (20 ounce) can pitted cherries	565 g
1 (20 ounce) can crushed pineapple, drained	565 g
1 (14 ounce) can sweetened condensed milk	395 g
1 cup miniature marshmallows	240 ml
1 cup pecans, chopped	240 ml
1 (8 ounce) carton whipped cream (topping)	225 g

- In large bowl, combine cherries, pineapple, sweetened condensed milk, marshmallows and pecans.
- Fold in whipped cream (topping), chill and serve in pretty crystal bowl. Add a couple drops of red food colouring for a brighter colour.

Soft-Mint Salad

1 (6 ounce) box lime gelatine	170 g
1 (20 ounce) can crushed pineapple with juice	565 g
5 ounce miniature marshmallows	140 g
1 (8 ounce) carton whipped cream (topping)	225 g
1 (8 ounce) bag soft (butter) mints, crushed	225 g

- Pour dry gelatine over pineapple. Add marshmallows and set overnight.
- Fold in whipped cream (topping) and soft (butter) mints. Pour into 23 x 33-cm (9 x 13-inch) dish and freeze.

Divinity Salad

1 (6 ounce) package lemon gelatine	170 g
1 (8 ounce) package cream cheese, softened	225 g
¾ cup pecans, chopped	180 ml
1 (15 ounce) can crushed pineapple with juice	425 g
1 (8 ounce) carton whipped cream (topping)	225 g

- With mixer, blend gelatine with 1 cup (240 ml) boiling water until it dissolves.
- Add cream cheese, beat slowly and increase speed until smooth. Add pecans and pineapple and cool in refrigerator until nearly set. Fold in whipped cream (topping). Pour into 23 x 33-cm (9 x 13-inch) dish and refrigerate.

Cherry Cranberry Salad

1 (6 ounce) package cherry gelatine	170 g
1 (20 ounce) can pitted cherries	565 g
1 (16 ounce) can whole cranberry sauce	.5 kg

- In mixing bowl, combine cherry gelatine and 1 cup (240 ml) boiling water and mix until gelatine dissolves.
- Mix cherries and cranberry sauce into gelatine.
- Pour into 23 x 33-cm (9 x 13-inch) dish and refrigerate.

Devilled Eggs

6 eggs, hard-boiled	
2 tablespoons sweet pickle relish	30 ml
3 tablespoons mayonnaise	45 ml
½ teaspoon mustard	2 ml

- Peel eggs and cut in half lengthwise. Remove yolks and mash with fork.
- Add relish, mayonnaise and mustard to yolks and place yolk mixture back into egg white halves.
- Sprinkle with paprika, if you like.

Sunshine Salad

2 (15 ounce) cans corn kernels (sweetcorn), drained	2 (425 g)
1 cup red and green capsicum (peppers), diced	240 ml
2 (15 ounce) cans peas, drained	2 (425 g)
1 (15 ounce) can kidney beans, rinsed, drained	425 g
Chilli powder, to taste	
1 (8 ounce) bottle Italian salad dressing	240 ml

- In large bowl, combine corn, capsicum (peppers), chilli, peas and beans.
- Pour dressing over vegetables and chill for several hours before serving.

Swiss Salad

1 large head cos (romaine) lettuce
1 bunch spring (green) onions with tops, chopped
8 ounce Swiss cheese, shredded 225 g
½ cup sunflower seeds, toasted 120 ml

- Tear lettuce into bite-size pieces. Add onions, cheese and sunflower seeds and toss.
- Serve with vinaigrette salad dressing.

Vinaigrette for Swiss Salad:
⅔ cup salad oil (such as canola or sunflower oil) 160 ml
⅓ cup red wine vinegar 80 ml
1 tablespoon seasoned salt 15 ml

- Combine all ingredients and chill.

Carrot Salad

3 cups carrots, finely grated 710 ml
1 (8 ounce) can crushed pineapple, drained 225 g
4 tablespoons flaked coconut 60 ml
1 tablespoon sugar 15 ml
⅓ cup mayonnaise 80 ml

- Combine carrots, pineapple, coconut and sugar and mix well. Toss with mayonnaise and chill.

Stuffed Cucumber Slices

3 cucumbers, peeled	
6 ounce cream cheese, softened	170 g
¼ cup stuffed green olives, chopped	60 ml
½ teaspoon seasoned salt	2 ml

- Halve cucumbers lengthwise and scoop out seeds.
- Beat cream cheese with mixer until creamy and add olives and seasoned salt. Fill hollows of cucumbers with cream cheese mixture.
- Press halves back together, wrap tightly in plastic wrap and chill.
- Remove plastic wrap and cut crosswise in .8-cm (⅓-inch) slices to serve.

Broccoli-Waldorf Salad

6 cups fresh broccoli florets	1.5 L
1 large red apple with peel, chopped	
½ cup sultanas (golden raisins)	120 ml
½ cup pecans, chopped	120 ml
½ cup prepared coleslaw dressing	120 ml

- In large bowl, combine broccoli, apple, sultanas (golden raisins) and pecans. Drizzle with dressing, toss to coat and refrigerate.

Colour-Coded Salad

1 (16 ounce) package tri-coloured macaroni, cooked, drained	.5 kg
1 red capsicum (pepper), cut into julienne strips	
1 cup zucchini (courgette), chopped	240 ml
1 cup broccoli florets	240 ml
1 cup Caesar salad dressing	240 ml

- Combine all ingredients. Toss with salad dressing and chill.

Nutty Cranberry Relish

1 pound fresh cranberries	.5 kg
2¼ cups sugar	540 ml
1 cup pecans, chopped, toasted	240 ml
1 cup orange marmalade	240 ml

- Preheat oven to 180° C (350° F).
- Wash and drain cranberries and mix with sugar.
- Place in 1-L (1-quart) baking dish, cover and bake for 1 hour.
- Add marmalade and pecans to cranberry mixture. Mix well, pour into container and chill before serving.

Pineapple-Vanilla Salad or Dessert

1 (20 ounce) can crushed pineapple with juice	570 g
1 (3 ounce) package instant vanilla pudding	85 g
2 cups miniature marshmallows	480 ml
1 cup pecans, chopped	240 ml
1 (8 ounce) carton whipped cream (topping)	225 g

- Place pineapple in large bowl and sprinkle with dry pudding mix.
- Add marshmallows and pecans and fold in whipped cream (topping). Pour into serving dish and chill.

Broccoli-Chicken Salad

3–4 boneless, skinless chicken breast halves, cooked, cubed	
2 cups fresh broccoli florets	480 ml
1 sweet red capsicum (pepper), seeded, chopped	
1 cup celery, chopped	240 ml
Honey-mustard salad dressing	

- Combine all ingredients.
- Toss mixture with honey-mustard salad dressing and chill.

Cottage Cheese-Fruit Salad

1 (6 ounce) package orange gelatine	170 g
1 (16 ounce) carton cottage cheese	.5 kg
22 ounce mandarine pieces (tidbits), drained	620 g
1 (20 ounce) can pineapple pieces (tidbits), drained	565 g
1 (8 ounce) carton whipped cream (topping)	225 g

- Sprinkle gelatine over cottage cheese and mix well.
- Add mandarine and pineapple and mix well. Fold in whipped cream (topping), chill and serve.

Pink Salad

1 (6 ounce) package raspberry gelatine	170 g
1 (20 ounce) can crushed pineapple with juice	565 g
1 cup cream-style cottage cheese	240 ml
1 (8 ounce) carton whipped cream (topping)	225 g
¼ cup pecans, chopped	60 ml

- Place gelatine in large bowl.
- Combine juice from pineapple and, if necessary, enough water to make 1¼ cups (300 ml) liquid. Heat, pour over gelatine and mix well.
- Cool in refrigerator just until gelatine begins to thicken. Fold in cottage cheese, whipped topping and pecans.
- Pour into moulds or 23 x 33-cm (9 x 13-inch) dish and refrigerate.

Cranapple Wiggle

A family friend made this recipe a tradition.

1 (6 ounce) package cherry gelatine	**170 g**
1 (16 ounce) can whole cranberry sauce	**.5 kg**
1 (15 ounce) can crushed pineapple with juice	**425 g**
1 cup apples, chopped	**240 ml**
1 cup pecans, chopped	**240 ml**

- Dissolve gelatine in 1½ cups (360 ml) boiling water and mix well.
- Add cranberry sauce, pineapple, apples and pecans.
- Pour into sprayed 23 x 33-cm (9 x 13-inch) glass dish and chill. Stir about the time it begins to set so the apples do not all stay on top. Serves 12.

Apple-Pineapple Salad

1 (6 ounce) package lemon gelatine	**170 g**
1 (15 ounce) can pineapple pieces (tidbits) with juice	**425 g**
1 cup apples with peel, diced	**240 ml**
1 cup pecans, chopped	**240 ml**

- Dissolve gelatine in 1 cup (240 ml) boiling water.
- Add pineapple and place in refrigerator until slightly thick. Fold in apples and pecans.
- Pour into solid mould or 18 x 28-cm (7 x 11-inch) dish and chill until firm.

Frozen Holiday Salad

6 ounce cream cheese, softened	170 g
3 tablespoons mayonnaise	45 ml
¼ cup sugar	60 ml
1 (16 ounce) can whole cranberry sauce	.5 kg
1 (8 ounce) can crushed pineapple, drained	225 g
1 cup pecans, chopped	240 ml
1 cup tiny marshmallows	240 ml
1 (8 ounce) carton whipped cream (topping)	225 g

- Cream the cheese, mayonnaise and sugar.
- Add fruit, pecans and marshmallows and fold in whipped cream (topping).
- Pour into sprayed 23 x 33-cm (9 x 13-inch) shallow glass dish and freeze.
- When ready to serve, take salad out of freezer a few minutes before cutting into squares.

Frozen Dessert Salad

1 (8 ounce) package cream cheese, softened	**225 g**
1 cup icing (powdered) sugar	**240 ml**
10 ounce strawberries, quartered	**280 g**
1 (15 ounce) can crushed pineapple, drained	**425 g**
1 (8 ounce) carton whipped cream (topping)	**225 g**

- In mixing bowl, beat cream cheese and sugar and fold in strawberries, pineapple and whipped cream (topping). (This will be even better if you stir in ¾ cup/180 ml chopped pecans.)
- Pour into 23 x 23-cm (9 x 9-inch) pan and freeze.
- Cut into squares to serve.

If stored in an airtight container, pecans will stay fresh for 6 months in the pantry or up to a year in the freezer!

Veggie Salad

Crunchy and good!

5 zucchini (courgette), sliced paper thin	
4 yellow squash, sliced paper thin	
1 head cauliflower, cut in bite-size pieces	
1 red capsicum (pepper), chopped	
1 bunch spring (green) onions with tops, sliced	
4 ounce slivered almonds, toasted	110 g
1 (8 ounce) bottle creamy Italian dressing	240 ml

- Mix zucchini (courgette), yellow squash, cauliflower, capsicum (pepper), onions, almonds, ½ teaspoon (2 ml) salt and ¼ teaspoon (1 ml) pepper.
- Add dressing and toss. Chill several hours before serving.

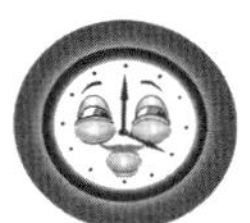

SIDE DISHES

Cheddar Potatoes

1 (10 ounce) jar processed cheese spread	280 g
⅓ cup sour cream	80 ml
2 spring (green) onions with tops, chopped	
3 cups instant seasoned mashed potatoes, prepared	710 ml

- Preheat oven to 180° C (350° F).
- In saucepan, heat cheese spread and add sour cream, onion and a little black pepper. Stir in potatoes and blend well.
- Pour into sprayed 2-L (2-quart) baking dish and cook for 25 minutes.

Mashed Potatoes Supreme

1 (8 ounce) package cream cheese, softened	225 g
½ cup sour cream	120 ml
2 tablespoons butter, softened	30 ml
1 (1 ounce) packet French onion soup mix	30 g
6–8 cups warm instant mashed potatoes	1.5–2 L

- Preheat oven to 180° C (350° F).
- With mixer, combine cream cheese, sour cream, butter and soup mix and mix well. Add potatoes and stir well.
- Transfer to 2-L (2-quart) baking dish and bake for 25 minutes or until hot throughout.

Potatoes Supreme

1 (32 ounce) package hash browns, shredded	1 kg
1 onion, chopped	
2 (10 ounce) cans cream of chicken soup	2 (280 g)
1 (8 ounce) carton sour cream	225 g

- Preheat oven to 180° C (350° F).
- In large bowl, combine all ingredients and mix well.
- Pour into sprayed 23 x 33-cm (9 x 13-inch) baking dish. Bake covered for 1 hour.

Tip: Sprinkle ½ cup (120 ml) parmesan or cheddar cheese on top for the last 5 minutes of baking.

Potatoes au Gratin

8 ounce processed cheese, cubed	225 g
16 ounce unthickened (half-and-half) cream	500 ml
1 cup cheddar cheese, shredded	240 ml
½ cup butter	120 ml
1 (32 ounce) package hash browns, shredded	1 kg

- Preheat oven to 180° C (350° F). In bain-marie (double boiler), melt processed cheese, cream, cheddar cheese and butter. Place hash browns in sprayed 23 x 33-cm (9 x 13-inch) baking dish and pour cheese mixture over potatoes. Bake uncovered for 1 hour.

Oven Fries

5 medium baking potatoes	
⅓ cup oil	80 ml
¾ teaspoon seasoned salt	4 ml
Paprika	

- Preheat oven to 190° C (375° F). Scrub potatoes, cut each in 6 lengthwise wedges and place in shallow baking dish.
- Combine oil, ¼ teaspoon (1 ml) pepper and seasoned salt and brush potatoes with mixture. Sprinkle potatoes lightly with paprika.
- Bake for about 50 minutes or until potatoes are tender and light brown. Baste twice with remaining oil mixture while baking.

Sweet Potatoes and Pecans

2 cups sweet potatoes, chopped, cooked	480 ml
1½ cups brown sugar	360 ml
¼ cup butter, melted	60 ml
1 cup pecans, chopped	240 ml

- Preheat oven to 180° C (350° F). Place half sweet potatoes in sprayed 2-L (2-quart) baking dish.
- Combine brown sugar, butter and pecans and sprinkle half mixture over sweet potatoes. Repeat layers and bake uncovered for 30 minutes.

Scalloped Potatoes

6 medium potatoes
½ cup butter 120 ml
1 tablespoon plain (all-purpose) flour 15 ml
2 cups cheddar cheese, shredded 480 ml
¾ cup milk 180 ml

- Preheat oven to 180° C (350° F).
- Peel and slice potatoes.
- Place half potatoes in sprayed 3-L (3-quart) baking dish. Slice half butter over potatoes, sprinkle with half flour and cover with half cheese.
- Repeat layers with cheese on top. Pour milk over casserole and sprinkle with a little pepper. (Prepare potatoes as fast as you can so they do not turn dark.)
- Cover and bake for 1 hour.

Twice-Baked Potatoes

8 medium baking potatoes	
2 tablespoons butter	30 ml
1 (10 ounce) jar processed cheese spread	280 g
1 tablespoon chopped dried chives	15 ml

- Bake potatoes at 180° C (350° F) for 1 hour or until done.
- Cut potatoes in half lengthwise, scoop flesh from potatoes and leave thin shell.
- With mixer, whip potato flesh with butter and ½ teaspoon (2 ml) salt.
- Gradually add cheese and chives and beat until light and fluffy.
- Spoon mixture into potato skin shells and sprinkle with paprika.
- Bake at 220° C (425° F) for 15 minutes.

Pasta with Basil

2½ cups small tube pasta	600 ml
1 small onion, chopped	
2 tablespoons oil	30 ml
2½ tablespoons dried basil	35 ml
1 cup mozzarella cheese, shredded	240 ml

- Cook pasta according to package directions.
- In frying pan (skillet), saute onion in oil.
- Stir in basil, 1 teaspoon (5 ml) salt and ¼ teaspoon (1 ml) pepper, cook and stir 1 minute.
- Drain pasta and add to basil mixture. (Leave about ½ cup water so pasta won't be too dry.)
- Remove from heat and stir in cheese just until it begins to melt.
- Serve immediately.

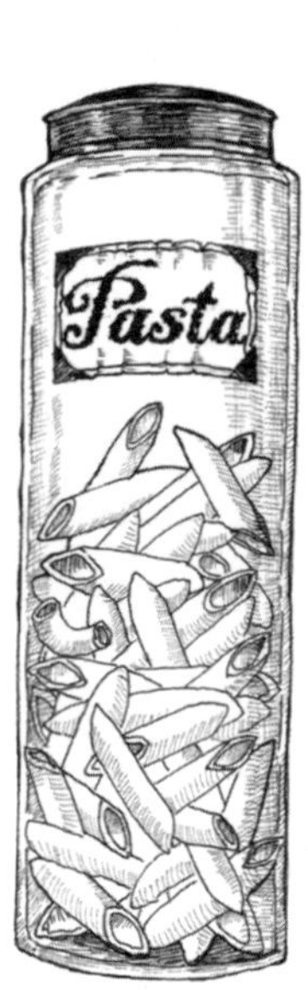

Creamy Fettuccine

1 (8 ounce) package fettuccine	225 g
1 pound Italian sausage	.5 kg
1 (10 ounce) can cream of mushroom soup	280 g
1 (16 ounce) carton sour cream	.5 kg

- Preheat oven to 160° C (325° F).
- Cook fettuccine according to package directions and drain.
- Cut sausage into 2.5-cm (1-inch) pieces, brown over medium heat, cook for 8 minutes and drain.
- Combine all ingredients and pour into sprayed 2-L (2-quart) baking dish.
- Bake for about 20 minutes or until bubbly.

Macaroni and Cheese

1 cup macaroni	240 ml
1½ cups cottage cheese	360 ml
1½ cup cheddar cheese, shredded	360 ml
4 tablespoons parmesan cheese, grated	60 ml

- Preheat oven to 180° C (350° F).
- Cook macaroni according to package directions and drain. Combine all cheeses and add macaroni to cheese mixture. Spoon into sprayed 2-L (2-quart) baking dish.
- Bake covered for 35 minutes.

Green Chilli-Rice

1 cup cooked instant rice	240 ml
1 (12 ounce) package cheddar cheese, shredded	340 g
1 (7 ounce) jar chopped green chillies	200 g
2 (8 ounce) cartons sour cream	2 (225 g)
½ teaspoon garlic powder	2 ml

- Preheat oven to 180° C (350° F).
- In large bowl, combine and mix all ingredients and add a little salt, if you like.
- Spoon into sprayed 23 x 33-cm (9 x 13-inch) baking dish and bake for 30 minutes.

Baked Rice

2 cups rice	480 ml
½ cup butter, melted	120 ml
1 (10 ounce) can cream of celery soup	280 g
1 (10 ounce) can French onion soup	280 g

- Preheat oven to 180° C (350° F).
- Combine all ingredients plus 1½ cups (360 ml) water and mix well.
- Pour into sprayed 3-L (3-quart) baking dish and bake covered for 1 hour.

Roasted Vegetables

1½ pounds assorted fresh vegetables	.7 kg
1 (11 ounce) can water chestnuts, drained	310 g
1 (1 ounce) packet French onion soup mix	30 g
2 tablespoons butter, melted	30 ml

- Preheat oven to 200° C (400° F).
- Cut all vegetables in uniform 5-cm (2-inch) pieces and place in sprayed 2-L (2-quart) baking dish with water chestnuts.
- Combine melted butter and soup mix, drizzle mixture over vegetables and stir well.
- Cover and bake vegetables for 20 to 25 minutes or until tender and stir once.
- Use your favourite vegetables such as squash, carrots, zucchini (courgettes), cauliflower or broccoli.

Buttered Vegetables

½ cup butter	120 ml
2 yellow squash, sliced	
16 ounce broccoli florets	.5 kg
10 ounce frozen corn kernels (sweetcorn)	280 g

- Melt butter in frying pan and combine all vegetables.
- Saute vegetables for 10 to 15 minutes or until tender but crisp. Add a little salt and serve warm.

Creamy Corn Casserole

½ cup butter	120 ml
1 (8 ounce) package cream cheese	225 g
3 (16 ounce) cans corn kernels (sweetcorn), drained	1.35 kg
1 (4 ounce) jar chopped green chillies	115 g
1½ cups biscuit (cracker) crumbs	360 ml

- Preheat oven to 180° C (350° F).
- Melt butter in saucepan, stir in cream cheese and mix until cream cheese melts.
- Add corn and chillies (and some salt and pepper, if you like), mix and pour into sprayed baking dish.
- Sprinkle biscuit (cracker) crumbs over casserole and bake for 25 minutes.

Fantastic Fried Corn

32 ounce frozen corn kernels (sweetcorn)	1 kg
½ cup butter	120 ml
1 cup thickened (whipping) cream	240 ml
1 tablespoon sugar	15 ml

- Place corn in large frying pan (skillet) over medium heat and add butter, cream, sugar and 1 teaspoon (5 ml) salt.
- Stir constantly and heat until most of cream and butter absorbs into corn.

Tasty Black-Eyed Peas

2 (10 ounce) packages frozen black-eyed peas	2 (280 g)
1¼ cups green capsicum (pepper), chopped	300 ml
¾ cup onion, chopped	180 ml
3 tablespoons butter	45 ml
1 (15 ounce) can stewed tomatoes with liquid	425 g

- Soak black-eyed peas overnight, then cook according to package directions and drain.
- Saute green capsicum (pepper) and onion in butter. Add peas, tomatoes and a little salt and pepper. Cook over low heat until thoroughly hot and stir often.

Creamed Green Peas

1 (16 ounce) package frozen green peas	.5 kg
2 tablespoons butter	30 ml
1 (10 ounce) can cream of celery soup	280 g
3 ounce cream cheese	85 g
1 (8 ounce) can water chestnuts, drained	230 g

- Steam peas on cooktop or in microwave until heated through.
- In large saucepan, combine butter, soup and cream cheese, cook on medium heat and stir until butter and cream cheese melt.
- Add peas and water chestnuts and mix. Serve hot.

Baked Onions

4 large onions, thinly sliced	
1½ cups potato chips, crushed	360 ml
1 cup cheddar cheese, shredded	240 ml
1 (10 ounce) can cream of chicken soup	280 g

- Preheat oven to 150° C (300° F).
- In 23 x 33-cm (9 x 13-inch) baking dish, alternate layers of onion, potato chips and cheese.
- Spoon soup over last layer and pour ¼ cup (60 ml) milk or water over top.
- Sprinkle with a little cayenne or black pepper and bake for 1 hour.

Creamy Cabbage Bake

1 head cabbage, shredded	
1 (10 ounce) can cream of celery soup	280 g
⅔ cup milk	160 ml
8 ounce cheddar cheese, shredded	225 g

- Preheat oven to 160° C (325° F).
- Place cabbage in sprayed 2-L (2-quart) baking dish.
- Dilute celery soup with milk and pour over cabbage.
- Bake covered for 30 minutes.
- Remove from oven, sprinkle with cheese and bake uncovered additional 5 minutes.

Brown Sugar Carrots

2 (15 ounce) cans carrots	2 (425 g)
¼ cup butter	60 ml
3 tablespoons brown sugar	45 ml
1 teaspoon ground ginger	5 ml

- Drain carrots and reserve 2 tablespoons (30 ml) liquid.
- Combine reserved liquid with butter, brown sugar and ginger and heat thoroughly.
- Add carrots, stir gently and cook for 3 minutes.
- Serve hot.

Pine Nut Green Beans

1 (16 ounce) package frozen green beans	.5 kg
¼ cup butter	60 ml
¾ cup pine nuts	180 ml
¼ teaspoon garlic powder	1 ml

- Cook beans in water in covered 3-L (3-quart) saucepan for 10 to 15 minutes or until tender but crisp then drain.
- Melt butter in frying pan (skillet) over medium heat, add pine nuts and cook, stirring frequently, until golden.
- Add pine nuts to green beans and sprinkle with a little salt and pepper. Serve hot.

Parmesan Broccoli

1 (16 ounce) package frozen broccoli spears	.5 kg
½ teaspoon garlic powder	2 ml
½ cup breadcrumbs	120 ml
¼ cup butter, melted	60 ml
½ cup parmesan cheese	120 ml

- Cook broccoli as directed on package and drain.
- Add garlic powder, breadcrumbs, butter and cheese (and some salt, if you like) and toss.
- Heat in microwave on high for 1 minute and serve.

Crunchy Broccoli

2 (10 ounce) packages frozen broccoli florets	2 (280 g)
1 (8 ounce) can sliced water chestnuts, drained, chopped	225 g
½ cup butter, melted	120 ml
1 (1 ounce) packet dry onion soup mix	30 g

- Place broccoli in microwave-safe dish, cover and microwave for 5 minutes.
- Stir broccoli and cook another 4 minutes.
- Add water chestnuts.
- Combine melted butter and soup mix, blend well and toss with broccoli.

Broccoli-Stuffed Tomatoes

4 medium tomatoes	
1 (10 ounce) package frozen chopped broccoli	280 g
6 ounce creamy garlic cheese, softened	170 g
½ teaspoon garlic salt	2 ml

- Preheat oven to 190° C (375° F).
- Cut tops off tomatoes and scoop out pulp.
- Cook broccoli according to package directions and drain well. Combine broccoli, cheese and garlic salt and heat just until cheese melts.
- Stuff broccoli mixture into tomatoes and place on baking tray (sheet). Bake for about 10 minutes.

Baked Tomatoes

2 (14 ounce) cans diced tomatoes, drained	2 (395 g)
1½ cups breadcrumbs, toasted, divided	360 ml
Scant ¼ cup sugar	60 ml
½ onion, chopped	
¼ cup butter, melted	60 ml

- Preheat oven to 160° C (325° F).
- Combine tomatoes, 1 cup (240 ml) breadcrumbs, sugar, onion and butter. Pour into sprayed baking dish and cover with remaining ½ cup (120 ml) breadcrumbs. Bake for 25 to 30 minutes or until crumbs are light brown.

Baked Eggplant

1 medium eggplant	
¼ cup butter, melted	60 ml
1 (5 ounce) can evaporated milk	145 g
1½ cups biscuit (cracker) crumbs	360 ml

- Preheat oven to 180° C (350° F).
- Peel, slice and boil eggplant until easily mashed, and drain.
- Season with a little salt and pepper and add butter, evaporated milk and crumbs.
- Pour into sprayed 2-L (2-quart) baking dish and bake for 25 minutes.

Fried Vegetable and Cheese Balls

3 large zucchini (courgettes), grated	
5 eggs	
1 tube round, buttery biscuits (crackers), crushed	340 g
½ cup parmesan cheese, grated	120 ml

- Combine zucchini (courgettes), eggs and biscuit (cracker) crumbs and mix well. Add cheese and a little salt and pepper.
- Drop by spoonfuls into frying pan (skillet) with a little oil.
- Fry for 15 minutes and brown on each side.

TIP: One tube round buttery crackers is one-third of 1 340 g (12 ounce) box.

Baked Pumpkin

5 cups cooked pumpkin (squash), drained	1.2 L
¾ cup cheddar cheese, shredded	180 ml
1 (10 ounce) can cream of chicken soup	280 g
1 (6 ounce) box herb stuffing (dressing) mix	170 g

- Preheat oven to 190° C (375° F).
- Place cooked pumpkin (squash) in mixing bowl and season with a little salt. Add cheese and soup and blend well.
- Place half stuffing mix (dressing) in sprayed 23 x 33-cm (9 x 13-inch) baking dish.
- Spoon in pumpkin mixture and sprinkle remaining stuffing mix on top.
- Bake uncovered for 30 minutes.

Chilli-Cheese Squash

1 pound yellow squash	.5 kg
⅔ cup mayonnaise	160 ml
1 (4 ounce) jar diced green chillies, drained	115 g
⅔ cup mild cheddar cheese, shredded	160 ml
⅔ cup breadcrumbs	160 ml

- Cook squash in salted water until tender but crisp and drain.
- Return squash to saucepan and stir in mayonnaise, chillies, cheese and breadcrumbs. Serve hot.

Stuffed Yellow Squash

5 large yellow squash	
1 (16 ounce) package frozen chopped spinach	.5 kg
1 (8 ounce) package cream cheese, cubed	225 g
1 (1 ounce) packet dry onion soup mix	30 g
Cheddar cheese, shredded	

- Preheat oven to 160° C (325° F). Steam squash whole until tender. Slit squash lengthwise and remove seeds with spoon.
- Cook spinach according to package directions and drain well. Add cream cheese to cooked spinach and stir until it melts. (Do not let boil.)
- Add soup mix and blend well. Fill scooped-out squash shells with spinach mixture and top with a few sprinkles cheese. Place on baking tray (sheet) and bake for 15 minutes.

Cheese Vegetable Bake

4 cups grated zucchini (courgettes)	1 L
1½ cups cheddar cheese, shredded	360 ml
4 eggs, beaten	
2 cups cheese biscuit (cracker) crumbs	480 ml

- Preheat oven to 180° C (350° F).
- In bowl, combine zucchini (courgettes), cheese and eggs and mix well. Spoon into sprayed 3-L (3-quart) baking dish and sprinkle biscuit (cracker) crumbs over top.
- Bake uncovered for 35 minutes.

Creamed-Spinach Bake

2 (10 ounce) packages frozen chopped spinach	2 (280 g)
6 ounce cream cheese, softened	170 g
3 tablespoons butter	45 ml
1 cup seasoned breadcrumbs	240 ml

- Preheat oven to 180° C (350° F).
- Cook spinach according to package directions and drain.
- Combine cream cheese and butter with spinach. Heat until they melt and mix well with spinach.
- Pour into sprayed 2-L (2-quart) baking dish and sprinkle a little salt over spinach.
- Cover with breadcrumbs and bake for 15 to 20 minutes.

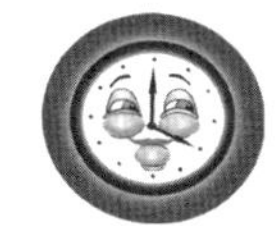

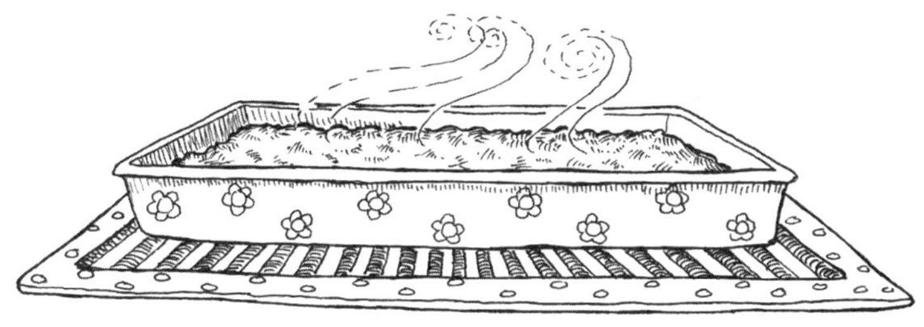

Spinach Casserole

1 (16 ounce) package frozen chopped spinach .5 kg
1 (8 ounce) package cream cheese with chives 225 g
1 (10 ounce) can cream of mushroom soup 280 g
1 egg, beaten
Biscuit (cracker) crumbs

- Preheat oven to 180° C (350° F).
- Cook spinach according to package directions and drain.
- Blend cream cheese and soup with egg, mix with spinach and pour into sprayed 2-L (2-quart) baking dish.
- Top with biscuit (cracker) crumbs and bake for 35 minutes.

Savoury Cauliflower

1 head cauliflower
1 (1 ounce) package hollandaise sauce mix 30 g
Fresh parsley
Lemon slices, optional

- Cut cauliflower into small florets and cook in salted water until barely tender. (Be very careful not to overcook cauliflower.)
- Mix sauce according to package directions.
- Drain cauliflower, top with sauce and sprinkle with parsley. Garnish with lemon slices, if you like.

Cauliflower Medley

1 head cauliflower, cut into florets
1 (14 ounce) can Italian stewed tomatoes with juice — 395 g
1 capsicum (pepper), chopped
1 onion, chopped
¼ cup butter — 60 ml
1 cup cheddar cheese, shredded — 240 ml

- Preheat oven to 180° C (350° F).
- Place cauliflower, stewed tomatoes, capsicum (pepper), onion and butter in large saucepan with about 2 tablespoons (30 ml) water and some salt and pepper.
- Cook in saucepan with lid until cauliflower is done, about 10 to 15 minutes. (Do not let cauliflower get mushy.)
- Place in 2-L (2-quart) baking dish and sprinkle cheese on top.
- Bake just until cheese melts.

Asparagus Bake

4 (10 ounce) cans asparagus	4 (280 g)
3 eggs, hard-boiled, sliced	
⅓ cup milk	80 ml
1½ cups cheddar cheese, shredded	360 ml
1¼ cups cheese biscuit (cracker) crumbs	300 ml

- Preheat oven to 180° C (350° F).
- Place asparagus in 18 x 28-cm (7 x 11-inch) baking dish, layer hard-boiled eggs on top and pour milk over casserole.
- Sprinkle cheese on top and add biscuit (cracker) crumbs.
- Bake, uncovered, for 30 minutes.

Sesame Asparagus

6 fresh asparagus spears, trimmed	
1 tablespoon butter	15 ml
1 teaspoon lemon juice	5 ml
1 teaspoon sesame seeds	5 ml

- Place asparagus in frying pan (skillet), sprinkle with salt if desired, add ¼ cup (60 ml) water and bring to a boil.
- Reduce heat, cover and simmer for 4 minutes.
- Melt butter and add lemon juice and sesame seeds.
- Drain asparagus and drizzle with butter mixture.

Baked Beans

2 (15 ounce) cans baked beans with ham, slightly drained	2 (425 g)
½ onion, finely chopped	
⅔ cup brown sugar	160 ml
¼ cup chilli sauce	60 ml
1 tablespoon Worcestershire sauce	15 ml
2 strips bacon	

- Preheat oven to 160° C (325° F).
- In bowl, combine beans, onion, brown sugar, chilli sauce and Worcestershire. Pour into sprayed 2-L (2-quart) baking dish and place bacon strips over bean mixture.
- Bake uncovered for 50 minutes.

Creamy Vegetable Casserole

1 (16 ounce) package frozen broccoli, carrots and cauliflower	.5 kg
1 (10 ounce) can cream of mushroom soup	280 g
1 (8 ounce) carton cream cheese with herbs and garlic	225 g
1 cup seasoned croutons	240 ml

- Preheat oven to 190° C (375° F).
- Cook vegetables according to package directions, drain and place in large bowl.
- Place soup and cream cheese in saucepan and heat just enough to mix easily.
- Pour soup mixture into vegetable mixture, stir well and pour into 2-L (2-quart) baking dish.
- Sprinkle with croutons and bake uncovered for 25 minutes or until bubbly.

Corn Vegetable Medley

1 (10 ounce) can creamed (cream-style) corn	280 g
½ cup milk	120 ml
2 cups fresh broccoli florets	480 ml
2 cups cauliflower florets	480 ml
1 cup cheddar cheese, shredded	240 ml

- In saucepan over medium heat, heat corn and milk to boiling and stir often.
- Stir in broccoli and cauliflower florets and return to boiling.
- Reduce heat to low and cover. Cook 20 minutes or until vegetables are tender, and stir occasionally.
- Stir in cheese and heat until cheese melts.

Calico Corn

1 (16 ounce) package frozen corn kernels (sweetcorn)	.5 kg
1 capsicum (pepper), chopped	
⅓ cup celery, chopped	80 ml
1 (10 ounce) jar processed cheese spread	280 g

- Preheat oven to 180° C (350° F).
- Cook corn in microwave according to package directions and drain well. Add capsicum (pepper) and celery. Stir in cheese and mix well.
- Pour into sprayed 2-L (2-quart) baking dish and bake covered for 30 minutes.

BEEF

Cheesy Beefy Gnocchi

1 pound lean beef mince (ground mince)	.5 kg
1 (10 ounce) jar processed cheese spread	280 g
1 (10 ounce) can cream of tomato soup	280 g
2 cups gnocchi or shell pasta	480 ml

- In frying pan (skillet), cook beef until brown and drain.
- Add cheese, soup, pasta and 1½ cups (360 ml) water and bring mixture to a boil.
- Cover and cook over medium heat for 10 to 12 minutes or until pasta is done. Stir often.

Chilli Casserole

40 ounce prepared chilli con carne	1.1 kg
2 (4 ounce) jars chopped green chillies	2 (115 g)
1 (2 ounce) can sliced black (ripe) olives, drained	55 g
8 ounce cheddar cheese, shredded	225 g
2 cups corn (tortilla) chips, crushed	480 ml

- Preheat oven to 180° C (350° F).
- Combine all ingredients and transfer to sprayed 3-L (3-quart) baking dish.
- Bake uncovered for 35 minutes or until bubbly.

Potato-Beef Casserole

4 medium potatoes, peeled, sliced	
1¼ pounds lean beef mince (ground beef), browned, drained	565 g
1 (10 ounce) can cream of mushroom soup	280 g
1 (10 ounce) can vegetable beef soup	280 g

- Preheat oven to 180° C (350° F).
- In large bowl, combine all ingredients plus ½ teaspoon each of salt and pepper and transfer to sprayed 3-L (3-quart) baking dish.
- Bake covered for 1 hour 30 minutes or until potatoes are tender.

Casserole Supper

1 pound lean beef mince (ground mince)	.5 kg
¼ cup white rice	60 ml
1 (10 ounce) can French onion soup	280 g
3 ounce fried onion rings	85 g

- Preheat oven to 160° C (325° F).
- Brown beef, drain and place in sprayed 18 x 28-cm (7 x 11-inch) baking dish. Add rice, onion soup and ½ cup (120 ml) water.
- Cover and bake for 40 minutes. Uncover, sprinkle onion rings over top and return to oven for 10 minutes.

Steak-Bake Italiano

2 pounds lean round steak	1 kg
2 teaspoons Italian herb seasoning	10 ml
1 teaspoon garlic salt	5 ml
2 (15 ounce) cans stewed tomatoes	2 (425 g)

- Preheat oven to 160° C (325° F).
- Cut steak into serving-size pieces, brown in frying pan and place in 23 x 33-cm (9 x 13-inch) baking dish.
- Combine herb seasoning, garlic salt and stewed tomatoes, mix well and pour over steak pieces.
- Cover and bake for 1 hour.

Easy Chilli

2 pounds lean beef mince (ground mince)	1 kg
1 onion, chopped	
4 (16 ounce) cans Mexican chilli beans with liquid	4 (.5 kg)
1 (1 ounce) package chilli seasoning mix	30 g
1 (46 ounce) can tomato juice	1.35 L

- Cook beef and onion in large, heavy pan; stir until meat crumbles and drain.
- Stir in remaining ingredients. Bring mixture to a boil, reduce heat and simmer, and stir occasionally, for 2 hours.

Beef and Bean Pie

Ingredient	Metric
1 pound lean beef mince (ground mince)	.5 kg
1 onion, chopped	
2 (16 ounce) cans borlotti (pinto) beans with liquid	2 (.5 kg)
1 (10 ounce) can tomatoes with liquid	280 g
2 ounces green chilli, chopped	55 g
6 ounces fried onion rings	170 g

- Preheat oven to 180° C (350° F).
- In frying pan (skillet), brown beef and onion and drain.
- In 2-L (2-quart) baking dish, layer 1 can beans, beef-onion mixture and ½ can tomatoes and green chillies. Repeat layer.
- Top with onion rings and bake uncovered for 30 minutes.

Taco Pie

1½ pounds lean beef mince (ground mince)	.7 kg
½ green capsicum (pepper), chopped	
1 teaspoon oil	5 ml
1 (15 ounce) can tomatoes with chopped fresh coriander (cilantro) and lime juice added (to taste)	425 g
1 tablespoon chilli powder	15 ml
¼ teaspoon garlic powder	1 ml
1½ cups cheddar cheese, shredded	360 ml
6 ounce prepared polenta (cornmeal) muffin mix	170 g
1 egg	
⅔ cup milk	160 ml

- Preheat oven to 190° C (375° F).
- Brown beef and capsicum (pepper) in oil in large frying pan (skillet) and drain well.
- Add 2 ml (½ teaspoon) salt, tomatoes, 1 cup (240 ml) water, chilli powder and garlic powder. Cook on medium heat for about 10 minutes or until most of liquid is gone.
- Pour into sprayed 23 x 33-cm (9 x 13-inch) baking dish. Sprinkle cheese on top.
- Combine muffin mix, egg and milk and beat well. Pour over cheese.
- Bake for 25 minutes or until muffin mix is light brown.
- Remove from oven and let set about 10 minutes before serving.

Simple Spaghetti Bake

8 ounces spaghetti 230 g
1 pound lean beef mince (ground beef) .5 kg
1 green capsicum (pepper), finely chopped
1 onion, chopped
1 (10 ounce) can cream of tomato soup 280 g
1 (15 ounce) can tomato pasta sauce 425 g
2 teaspoons Italian seasoning 10 ml
1 (8 ounce) can corn kernels (sweetcorn), drained 225 g
1 (4 ounce) can black sliced olives, drained 115 g
12 ounce cheddar cheese, shredded 340 g

- Cook spaghetti according to package directions, drain and set aside.
- In frying pan (skillet), cook beef, capsicum (pepper) and onion and drain.
- Add remaining ingredients, ⅓ cup (120 ml) water, ½ teaspoon (2 ml) salt and spaghetti to beef mixture and stir well. Pour into sprayed 23 x 33-cm (9 x 13-inch) baking dish and cover.
- Refrigerate 2 to 3 hours, then preheat oven to 180° C (350° F).
- Bake covered for 45 minutes.

Easy Winter Warmer

This is such a good spaghetti sauce on noodles and is a great substitute for cream sauce.

1 (12 ounce) package medium egg noodles	**340 g**
3 tablespoons butter	**45 ml**
1½ pounds lean beef mince (ground beef)	**.7 kg**
½ cup onion, chopped	**120 ml**
½ cup capsicum (pepper), chopped	**120 ml**
1 (28 ounce) jar spaghetti sauce	**795 g**
12 ounce mozzarella cheese, shredded	**340 g**

- Preheat oven to 180° C (350° F).
- Cook noodles according to package directions in pot of boiling water with a dab of oil and salt. Drain thoroughly, add butter and stir until butter melts.
- Brown beef, onions and capsicum (peppers) and drain thoroughly.
- Pour half of spaghetti sauce in bottom of sprayed 23 x 33-cm (9 x 13-inch) baking dish.
- Layer half noodles, half beef and half cheese. Repeat for second layer.
- Bake covered for about 30 minutes or until dish is hot.

Pepper Steak

1¼ pound sirloin steak, cut in strips 565 g
Seasoned salt
1 cup onion, sliced 240 ml
1 cup capsicum (pepper), sliced 240 ml
1 (16 ounce) package cubed cheddar cheese with finely chopped jalapeños .5 kg

- Sprinkle steak with seasoned salt.
- Spray large frying pan (skillet) and cook steak strips for 10 minutes or until no longer pink.
- Remove steak from pan and set aside.
- Stir in vegetables and ½ cup water and simmer vegetables for 5 minutes or until all liquid cooks out.
- Add cheese and jalapenos and turn heat to medium-low.
- When cheese melts, stir in steak and serve over hot, cooked rice.

Ravioli and More

1 pound lean beef mince (ground beef)	.5 kg
1 teaspoon garlic powder	5 ml
1 large onion, chopped	
2 zucchini (courgettes), grated	
¼ cup butter	60 ml
1 (28 ounce) jar spaghetti sauce	795 g
1 (25 ounce) package cooked mushroom ravioli	710 g
12 ounce mozzarella cheese, shredded	340 g

- Preheat oven to 180° C (350° F).
- Brown beef in large frying pan (skillet) until no longer pink and drain. Add garlic powder and ½ teaspoon (2 ml) salt.
- In saucepan cook onion and zucchini (courgettes) in butter until tender but crisp and stir in spaghetti sauce.
- In sprayed 23 x 33-cm (9 x 13-inch) baking dish, spread ½ cup (120 ml) sauce. Layer half of ravioli, half spaghetti sauce, half beef and half cheese. Repeat layers, but omit remaining cheese. Cover and bake for 35 minutes.
- Uncover and sprinkle remaining cheese. Let stand 10 minutes before serving.

Asian Beef and Noodles

1¼ pounds beef mince (ground beef)	565 g
2 (3 ounce) packages oriental-flavoured ramen noodles	2 (85 g)
1 (16 ounce) package frozen stir-fry vegetable mixture	.5 kg
½ teaspoon ground ginger	2 ml
3 tablespoons thinly sliced spring (green) onions	45 ml

- In large frying pan (skillet), brown beef and drain.
- Add ½ cup (120 ml) water, a little salt and pepper, simmer 10 minutes and transfer to separate bowl.
- In same pan, combine 2 cups (480 ml) water, vegetables, noodles (broken up), ginger and both noodle seasoning packets.
- Bring to a boil and reduce heat.
- Cover, simmer 3 minutes or until noodles are tender and stir occasionally.
- Return beef to pan and stir in spring (green) onions. Serve right from pan.

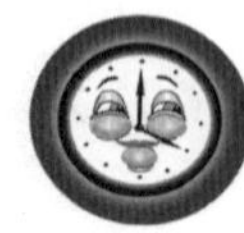

Shepherds' Pie

1 pound lean beef mince (ground beef)	.5 kg
1 (1 ounce) packet taco seasoning mix	30 g
1 cup cheddar cheese, shredded	240 ml
1 (11 ounce) can corn kernels (sweetcorn), drained	310 g
2 cups instant mashed potatoes, prepared	480 ml

- Preheat oven to 180° C (350° F).
- In frying pan (skillet), brown beef, cook 10 minutes, drain.
- Add taco seasoning and ¾ cup (180 ml) water and cook another 5 minutes. Spoon beef mixture into 20-cm (8-inch) baking pan and sprinkle cheese on top.
- Sprinkle with corn and spread mashed potatoes over top. Bake for 25 minutes or until top is golden.

Smothered Beef Patties

1½ pounds beef mince (ground beef)	.7 kg
½ cup chilli sauce	120 ml
½ cup round, buttery biscuit (cracker) crumbs	120 ml
14 ounce beef liquid stock (broth)	415 ml

- Combine beef, chilli sauce and biscuit (cracker) crumbs and form into 5 or 6 patties.
- In frying pan (skillet), brown patties, pour beef stock (broth) over patties and bring to a boil. Reduce heat, cover and simmer for 40 minutes.

Potato-Beef Bake

This is really good sprinkled with 1 cup shredded cheddar cheese.

1 pound beef mince (ground beef) .5 kg
1 (10 ounce) can tomato pasta sauce 280 g
1 (10 ounce) jar processed cheese spread with finely chopped jalapeño chillies 280 g
1 (32 ounce) package hash browns, shredded 1 kg

- Preheat oven to 200° C (400° F).
- In frying pan (skillet), cook beef over medium heat until no longer pink and drain.
- Add pasta sauce, cheese spread and jalapeños to beef and mix well.
- Place hash browns in sprayed 23 x 33-cm (9 x 13-inch) baking dish and top with beef mixture.
- Cover and bake for 25 minutes.
- Uncover and bake additional 10 minutes.

Delicious Meatloaf

1½ pounds lean beef mince (ground beef)	**.7 kg**
⅔ cup dry Italian-seasoned breadcrumbs	**160 ml**
1 (10 ounce) can mushroom soup, divided	**280 g**
2 eggs, beaten	
2 tablespoons butter	**30 ml**

- Preheat oven to 180° C (350° F).
- Mix beef, breadcrumbs, half mushroom soup and eggs thoroughly. In baking pan, shape firmly into 20 x 10-cm (8 x 4-inch) loaf and bake for 45 minutes.
- In small saucepan, mix butter, remaining soup and ¼ cup (60 ml) water, heat thoroughly and serve sauce over meatloaf.

Spanish Meatloaf

1½ pounds lean beef mince (ground beef)	**.7 kg**
2 cups cooked white rice	**480 ml**
1 egg, beaten	
¾ cup round, buttery biscuit (cracker) crumbs	**180 ml**
Chunky salsa	

- Preheat oven to 180° C (350° F).
- Combine beef, rice, egg and biscuit (cracker) crumbs and shape into loaf in sprayed pan. Bake for 1 hour. Serve meatloaf topped with salsa.

Baked Onion-Mushroom Steak

1½ pounds (½ inch) thick round steak	**.7 kg/1 cm**
1 (10 ounce) can cream of mushroom soup	**280 g**
1 (1 ounce) packet dry onion soup mix	**30 g**

- Preheat oven to 160° C (325° F).
- Place steak in sprayed 23 x 33-cm (9 x 13-inch) baking dish and sprinkle with a little salt and pepper.
- Pour mushroom soup and ½ cup (120 ml) water over steak and sprinkle with onion soup mix.
- Cover and bake for 2 hours.

Smothered Beef Steak

2 pounds lean round steak	**1 kg**
1 cup rice	**240 ml**
14 ounce beef liquid stock (broth)	**415 ml**
1 green capsicum (pepper), chopped	

- Cut steak into serving-size pieces and brown in very large frying pan (skillet).
- Add rice, beef stock (broth), capsicum (pepper) and 1 cup (240 ml) water to pan and bring to a boil.
- Reduce heat, cover and simmer for 1 hour.

Red Wine Round Steak

2 pounds (¾ inch) thick round steak	1 kg/2 cm
1 (1 ounce) packet dry onion soup mix	30 g
1 cup dry red wine	240 ml
4 ounce mushrooms, sliced	115 g

- Preheat oven to 160° C (325° F).
- Remove all fat from steak and cut into serving-size pieces. Brown meat in frying pan (skillet) with a little oil. When browned on both sides, place in sprayed 23 x 33-cm (9 x 13-inch) baking dish.
- In frying pan, combine soup mix, wine, mushrooms and 1 cup (240 ml) hot water and pour over steak. Cover and bake for 1 hour 20 minutes or until steak is tender.

Smothered Steak

2 pound round steak	1 kg
1 (10 ounce) can mushroom soup	280 g
1 (1 ounce) packet dry onion soup mix	30 g
⅔ cup milk	160 ml

- Preheat oven to 160° C (325° F). Cut steak into serving-size pieces and place in sprayed 23 x 33-cm (9 x 13-inch) baking pan.
- In saucepan, combine mushroom soup, soup mix and milk. Heat just enough to mix well and pour over steak. Seal with foil and bake for 1 hour.

Lean Mean Round Steak

Plain (all-purpose) flour	
1 teaspoon paprika	5 ml
2 pounds lean round steak, cut into strips	1kg
2 tablespoons oil	30 ml
1 cup onions, chopped	240 ml
½ cup green capsicum (pepper), chopped	120 ml
2 (15 ounce) cans tomatoes with chopped fresh coriander (cilantro) and lime juice added (to taste)	2 (425 g)
2 (8 ounce) cans tomato pasta sauce	2 (225 g)
1 tablespoon chilli powder	15 ml
Cheddar cheese, shredded	
Fresh coriander (cilantro)	

- Combine flour, paprika and a little salt and pepper in bowl. Dredge steak strips in flour and set aside.
- Heat oil in large, heavy frying pan (skillet) over medium heat. Brown meat and add onions, capsicum (peppers), tomatoes, tomato sauce, chilli powder and 1 cup (240 ml) water. Reduce heat to medium-low, cover and simmer for 1 hour.
- To serve, arrange steak on hot, ovenproof serving platter and cover with sauce. Sprinkle shredded cheese on top.
- Place under griller (broiler) for 1 to 2 minutes or until cheese melts. Garnish with fresh coriander (cilantro).
- Serve over hot, cooked rice. Serves 6 to 8.

Roasted Garlic Steak

2 (15 ounce) cans tomato soup with roasted garlic and herbs — 2 (425 g)
½ cup Italian salad dressing — 120 ml
1½ pounds (¾ inch) thick boneless beef sirloin steak — .7 kg/2 cm

- In saucepan, combine soup, salad dressing and ⅓ cup (80 ml) water.
- Grill (broil) steaks to desired result. (Allow 15 minutes for medium.) Turn once and brush often with sauce.
- Heat remaining sauce to serve with steak.

Pot Roast

4–6 pound chuck roast — 1.8 kg
1 (10 ounce) can French onion soup — 280 g
1 (1 ounce) packet dry onion soup mix — 30 g
4–6 potatoes, peeled, quartered

- Preheat oven to 180° C (350° F).
- Place roast on large sheet of heavy-duty foil.
- Combine soup and soup mix and spread over roast.
- Add potatoes and secure edges of foil tightly.
- Bake for 3 to 4 hours.

Slow Cookin', Good Tastin' Brisket

½ cup smoky (hickory) barbecue sauce	120 ml
4–5 pound beef brisket	1.8–2.2 kg
1 (5 ounce) bottle Worcestershire sauce	145 g
¾ cup barbecue sauce	180 ml

- Preheat oven to 135° C (275° F).
- Pour smoky (hickory) barbecue sauce over brisket, cover and chill overnight.
- Drain and pour Worcestershire sauce over brisket.
- Cover and bake for 6 to 7 hours.
- Cover with barbecue sauce and bake, uncovered, for additional 30 minutes.
- Slice very thinly across grain.

Next-Day Beef

1 (5–6 pound) trimmed beef brisket	**2.2–2.7 kg**
1 (1 ounce) packet dry onion soup mix	**30 g**
1 (10 ounce) bottle steak sauce	**280 g**
1 (12 ounce) bottle barbecue sauce	**340 g**

- Preheat oven to 160° C (325° F).
- Place brisket, cut side up, in roasting pan.
- In bowl, combine onion soup mix, steak and sauces and pour over brisket.
- Cover and cook for 4 to 5 hours or until tender.
- Remove brisket from pan, pour off drippings and chill both, separately, overnight.
- The next day, trim all fat from meat, slice and reheat.
- Skim fat off drippings, reheat and serve sauce over brisket.

CHICKEN

Deluxe Dinner Nachos

Nachos:

1 (14 ounce) package corn (tortilla) chips, divided	395 g
8 ounce processed cheese, shredded, divided	225 g
1 (8 ounce) can chopped jalapeños, divided	225 g

Deluxe Nacho Topping:

1 (11 ounce) can corn kernels (sweetcorn)	310 g
1 (15 ounce) can borlotti (pinto) beans, drained with chopped jalapeño chillies	425 g
2 cups roast (rotisserie) chicken, skinned, chopped	480 ml
1 bunch spring (green) onions, chopped	

- Place about three-quarters of corn (tortilla) chips in bottom of sprayed baking dish. Sprinkle half cheese and about 3 jalapeños on top. Heat at 200° C (400° F) just until cheese melts.
- Combine corn, beans, jalapeños and chicken in saucepan. Heat over medium heat, stirring constantly, until mixture is hot. Spoon mixture over nachos, place dish in oven and heat for about 10 minutes.
- Sprinkle remaining cheese and spring (green) onions over top and serve immediately. Garnish with remaining jalapeños, remaining corn chips and salsa.

Chucky Clucky Casserole

1 (16 ounce) package frozen broccoli	500 g
3 cups cooked chicken, diced	710 ml
1 (10 ounce) can cream of chicken soup	280 g
2 tablespoons milk	30 ml
⅓ cup mayonnaise	80 ml
2 teaspoons lemon juice	10 ml
3 tablespoons butter, melted	45 ml
1 cup breadcrumbs or biscuit (cracker) crumbs	240 ml
⅓ cup cheddar cheese, shredded	80 ml

- Preheat oven to 180° C (350° F).
- Cook broccoli according to package directions and drain. Place broccoli in sprayed 23 x 33-cm (9 x 13-inch) glass baking dish. Sprinkle 1 teaspoon (5 ml) salt over broccoli and cover with diced chicken.
- In saucepan, combine soup, milk, mayonnaise, lemon juice and ¼ teaspoon (1 ml) pepper. Heat just enough to thin soup a little and pour over chicken.
- Mix melted butter, breadcrumbs and cheese and sprinkle over soup mixture. Bake uncovered for 30 minutes or until mixture is hot and bubbly.

Chicken Chow Mein

3½ cups cooked chicken breasts, cubed	830 ml
2 (10 ounce) cans cream of chicken soup	2 (280 g)
2 (15 ounce) cans stir-fry vegetables, drained	2 (425 g)
1 (8 ounce) can sliced water chestnuts, drained	225 g
¾ cup cashew nuts, chopped	180 ml
1 green capsicum (pepper), chopped	
1 onion, chopped	
1 cup celery, chopped	240 ml
¼ teaspoon chilli (hot) sauce	1 ml
1¼ cups chow mein noodles	300 ml

- Preheat oven to 180° C (350° F).
- Combine chicken, soup, vegetables, water chestnuts, cashew nuts, green capsicum (pepper), onion, celery and hot sauce in large bowl. Stir to mix well.
- Spoon into sprayed 23 x 33-cm (9 x 13-inch) baking dish. Sprinkle chow mein noodles over top of casserole.
- Bake uncovered for 35 minutes or until bubbling at edges of casserole. Let set 5 minutes before serving.

Chicken Spaghetti

Ingredient	Metric
3 chicken breasts, boiled	
1 (10 ounce) can tomatoes	280 g
1 (2 ounce) jar green chillies	55 g
1 (10 ounce) can cream of mushroom soup	280 g
8 ounce cheddar cheese, shredded	225 g
8 ounce processed cheese, shredded	225 g
1 (12 ounce) package spaghetti	340 g

- Preheat oven to 180° C (350° F).
- Shred cooked chicken into large bowl. Add tomatoes, chillies, soup, and cheeses. Boil spaghetti according to package directions and drain.
- Add to chicken mixture; mix well. Pour into 3-L (3-quart) baking dish and bake for 35 minutes.

Alfredo Chicken

5–6 boneless, skinless chicken breast halves
16 ounce broccoli florets .5 kg
1 red capsicum (pepper), seeded, chopped
1 (16 ounce) jar alfredo sauce .5 kg

- Preheat oven to 160° C (325° F).
- Brown and cook chicken breasts in large frying pan (skillet) with a little oil until juices run clear. Transfer to sprayed 23 x 33-cm (9 x 13-inch) baking dish.
- Steam broccoli until cooked through and drain. Spoon broccoli and capsicum (pepper) over chicken.
- In small saucepan, heat alfredo sauce with ¼ cup (60 ml) water. Pour over chicken and vegetables. Cover and cook 15 to 20 minutes.
- *TIP: This chicken-broccoli dish can be 'dressed up' a bit by sprinkling shredded parmesan cheese on top after casserole bakes.*

Quick Russian Chicken

This is great when you don't have time to cook.

6 boneless, skinless chicken breast halves
1 (8 ounce) bottle Thousand Island (catalina) dressing — 225 g
1 (5 ounce) jar apricot jam — 145 g
1 (1 ounce) packet dry onion soup mix — 30 g

- Preheat oven to 180° C (350° F).
- Place chicken breasts in sprayed, shallow baking dish.
- Combine dressing, apricot jam, onion soup mix and ¼ cup (60 ml) water in saucepan and bring to a slow boil. Remove from heat and pour over chicken.
- Cover dish with foil and bake for 1 hour. Remove foil, baste with sauce and bake uncovered for additional 30 minutes. Serve immediately.

Aztec Creamy Salsa Chicken

6 boneless, skinless chicken breast halves
Oil

1 (1 ounce) packet dry taco seasoning mix	**30 g**
1 (16 ounce) jar salsa	**.5 kg**
1 (8 ounce) carton sour cream	**225 g**

- Preheat oven to 180° C (350° F).
- Brown chicken breasts in frying pan (skillet) and transfer to sprayed 23 x 33-cm (9 x 13-inch) baking dish. Sprinkle taco seasoning over chicken and top with salsa.
- Cover and bake for 35 minutes.
- Remove chicken to serving plates. Add sour cream to juices in pan, stir well and microwave on high for about 2 minutes. Stir pan juices and sour cream for sauce to serve over chicken.

Finger Lickin' BBQ Chicken

2 pound chicken, quartered	1 kg
½ cup tomato sauce (ketchup)	120 ml
¼ cup butter, melted	60 ml
2 tablespoons sugar	30 ml
1 tablespoon mustard	15 ml
½ teaspoon minced garlic	2 ml
¼ cup lemon juice	60 ml
¼ cup white vinegar	60 ml
¼ cup Worcestershire sauce	60 ml

- Preheat oven to 160° C (325° F).
- Sprinkle chicken quarters with salt and pepper and brown in frying pan (skillet). Place in sprayed baking pan.
- Combine tomato sauce (ketchup), butter, sugar, mustard, garlic, lemon juice, vinegar and Worcestershire. Pour over chicken, cover and bake for 50 minutes.

Parmesan Chicken Breasts

6 boneless, skinless chicken breast halves	
1½ cups dry breadcrumbs	360 ml
½ cup parmesan cheese, grated	120 ml
1 teaspoon dried basil	5 ml
½ teaspoon garlic powder	2 ml
1 (8 ounce) carton sour cream	225 g

- Preheat oven to 160° C (325° F).
- Flatten chicken to 1-cm (½-inch) thickness. Combine breadcrumbs, parmesan cheese, basil and garlic powder in shallow dish.
- Dip chicken in sour cream, coat with crumb mixture and place (so chicken breasts do not touch) in sprayed 25 x 38-cm (10 x 15-inch) baking dish.

- Bake uncovered for 50 to 60 minutes or until golden brown.

An easy way to get seasonings and spices to stick to chicken and roasts is to place them on plastic wrap, season well on all sides and roll meat in plastic wrap. By pressing seasonings into meat, they are more likely to stay on all sides. Remove wrap and cook.

Chilli-Chicken Roll-Ups

8 boneless, skinless chicken breast halves	
2 (4 ounce) jars diced green chillies	**2 (115 g)**
8 ounce cheddar cheese, shredded	**225 g**
½ cup butter, melted	**120 ml**
2 cups corn (tortilla) chips, crushed	**480 ml**

- Place each chicken breast on wax paper, flatten to about .5 cm (¼ inch) thickness with rolling pin or mallet and season with 1 teaspoon (5 ml) salt and ½ teaspoon (2 ml) pepper.
- Place diced green chillies and a little cheese evenly in centre of each chicken breast. Carefully roll each chicken breast so no chillies or cheese seep out and secure with toothpicks.
- Place each chicken in small casserole dish and chill several hours or overnight. When ready to bake, roll each chicken breast in melted butter and crushed corn (tortilla) chips.
- Bake at 180° C (350° F) for about 25 to 30 minutes or until tender.

Chicken Quesadillas

3 boneless, skinless chicken breast halves, cubed
1 (10 ounce) jar processed cheese spread 280 g
⅔ cup chunky salsa 160 ml
10 flour tortillas

- Preheat oven to 200° C (400° F).
- Cook chicken in frying pan (skillet) until juices evaporate and stir often. Add cheese and salsa and heat thoroughly.
- Spread about ⅓ cup (80 ml) soup mixture on half tortilla to within 1 cm (½ inch) of edge. Moisten edge with water, fold over and seal. Place tortillas on 2 baking trays (sheets). Bake for 5 to 6 minutes.

Cola Chicken

4–6 boneless, skinless chicken breast halves
1 cup tomato sauce (ketchup) 240 ml
1 cup cola 240 ml
2 tablespoons Worcestershire sauce 30 ml

- Preheat oven to 180° C (350° F).
- Place chicken in 23 x 33-cm (9 x 13-inch) baking dish and sprinkle with salt and pepper.
- Mix tomato sauce (ketchup), cola and Worcestershire sauce and pour over chicken. Cover and bake for 50 minutes.

Crunchy Chip Chicken

1½ cups sour cream potato chips, crushed	**360 ml**
1 tablespoon dried parsley	**15 ml**
1 egg, beaten	
1 tablespoon Worcestershire sauce	**15 ml**
4 large boneless, skinless chicken breast halves	
¼ cup oil	**60 ml**

- In shallow bowl, combine potato chips and parsley. In another shallow bowl, combine beaten egg, Worcestershire and 1 tablespoon water.
- Dip chicken pieces in egg mixture and dredge chicken in potato chip mixture. Heat oil in heavy frying pan (skillet) and fry chicken pieces in skillet for about 10 minutes.
- Turn each piece over and cook additional 10 minutes until golden brown or until juices run clear.

Cranberry Chicken

6 boneless, skinless chicken breast halves	
1 (16 ounce) can whole cranberry sauce	.5 kg
1 large tart apple, peeled, chopped	
⅓ cup walnuts, chopped	80 ml
1 teaspoon curry powder	5 ml

- Place chicken in sprayed 23 x 33-cm (9 x 13-inch) baking pan and bake uncovered at 180° C (350° F) for 20 minutes. Combine cranberry sauce, apple, walnuts and curry powder and spoon over chicken.
- Bake uncovered for additional 25 minutes or until chicken juices run clear.

Spicy Chicken and Rice

3 cups cooked chicken, sliced	710 ml
2 cups cooked brown rice	480 ml
1 (10 ounce) jar processed cheese spread	280 g
1 (10 ounce) can chopped tomatoes	280 g
1 (2 ounce) jar green chillies	55 g

- Preheat oven to 180° C (350° F).
- Combine chicken, rice, cheese spread, tomatoes and green chillies and mix well. Spoon mixture into sprayed 3-L (3-quart) baking dish.
- Cook covered for 45 minutes.

Crusted Chicken

½ cup parmesan cheese	120 ml
1½ cups cornflakes	360 ml
1 (1 ounce) packet French onion soup mix	30 g
2 pounds chicken drumsticks	1 kg
½ cup butter, melted	120 ml

- Preheat oven to 180° C (350° F).
- Combine cheese, cornflakes and soup mix.
- Dip washed, dried chicken in melted butter and dredge in cornflake mixture.
- Bake uncovered for 50 minutes or until golden brown.

Sunday Chicken

5–6 boneless, skinless chicken breast halves	
½ cup sour cream	120 ml
¼ cup soy sauce	60 ml
1 (10 ounce) can French onion soup	280 g

- Preheat oven to 180° C (350° F). Place chicken in sprayed 23 x 33-cm (9 x 13-inch) baking dish.
- In saucepan, combine sour cream, soy sauce and soup and heat just enough to mix well. Pour over chicken breasts.
- Bake covered for 55 minutes.

Chicken and Wild Rice Special

1 (6 ounce) package instant wild rice mix — 170 g
4–5 boneless, skinless chicken breast halves
2 (10 ounce) cans French onion soup — 2 (280 g)
1 red and 1 green capsicum (pepper), julienned

- In saucepan, cook rice according to package directions and keep warm. In large frying pan (skillet) with a little oil over medium-high heat, brown chicken breasts on both sides.
- Add soups, ¾ cup (180 ml) water and capsicum (peppers). Reduce heat to medium-low, cover and cook 15 minutes.
- To serve, place rice on serving platter with chicken breasts on top. Serve sauce in gravy boat to pour over chicken and rice.

TIP: For a thicker sauce, spoon 2 or 3 tablespoons (30 ml) sauce into small bowl and stir in 2 tablespoons (30 ml) flour. Mix well and stir in onion soup. Heat and stir constantly until sauce thickens.

Party Chicken Breasts

6–8 boneless, skinless chicken breast halves	
8 strips bacon	
1 (2.5 ounce) pack beef jerky (dried beef)	70 g
1 (10 ounce) can cream of chicken soup	280 g
1 (8 ounce) carton sour cream	225 g

- Preheat oven to 160° C (325° F).
- Wrap each chicken breast with 1 strip bacon and secure with toothpicks.
- Place beef jerky (dried beef) in bottom of shallow baking pan and top with chicken. Heat soup and sour cream, pour over chicken. Bake uncovered for 1 hour.

Lemon Chicken

6 boneless, skinless chicken breast halves	
6 ounces lemon juice cordial (lemonade)	170 g
⅓ cup soy sauce	80 ml
1 teaspoon garlic powder	5 ml

- Preheat oven to 180° C (350° F).
- Place chicken in sprayed 23 x 33-cm (9 x 13-inch) baking dish. Combine lemon cordial (lemonade), soy sauce and garlic powder and pour over chicken.
- Cover with foil and bake for 45 minutes. Uncover, pour juices over chicken and cook additional 10 minutes.

Dad's Best Smoked Chicken

3 whole chickens, cut in half	
½ cup butter	120 ml
2 teaspoons Worcestershire sauce	10 ml
2 dashes chilli (hot) sauce	
2 tablespoons lemon juice	30 ml
½ teaspoon garlic salt	2 ml
12 ounce lemon-lime carbonated drink	350 ml

- Sprinkle chickens with pepper and leave at room temperature for 1 hour. In small saucepan, melt butter and add Worcestershire sauce, chilli (hot) sauce, lemon juice, garlic salt and lemon-lime carbonated drink.
- Cook chickens over low charcoal fire with hickory or mesquite chips around sides of fire. Turn often and baste with sauce mixture several times.
- When chicken is done (about 60 minutes), baste once more to keep chicken moist.

Grilled Chicken Cordon Bleu

6 boneless, skinless chicken breast halves	
6 slices Swiss cheese	
6 thin slices deli ham	
3 tablespoons oil	45 ml
1 cup seasoned breadcrumbs	240 ml

- Flatten chicken to .5 cm (¼ inch) thickness and place 1 slice cheese and ham on each piece of chicken to within .5 cm (¼ inch) of edges.
- Fold in half and secure with toothpicks. Brush chicken with oil and roll in breadcrumbs. Grill, covered, over medium heat for 15 to 18 minutes or until juices run clear.

Italian Chicken and Rice

3 boneless, chicken breasts halves, cut into strips	
14 ounce chicken liquid stock (broth) seasoned with Italian herbs	415 ml
¾ cup rice	180 ml
¼ cup parmesan cheese, grated	60 ml

- Cook chicken in non-stick frying pan (skillet) until brown, stirring often, and set aside.
- Add stock (broth) and rice to pan and heat to boil. Cover and simmer over low heat for 25 minutes. (Add water if needed.) Stir in cheese and return chicken to pan. Cover and cook for 5 minutes or until done.

Lemony Chicken and Noodles

1 (8 ounce) package wide egg noodles	225 g
10 ounce sugar snap peas (pea pods)	280 g
14 ounce chicken liquid stock (broth)	415 ml
1 teaspoon fresh grated lemon peel	5 ml
2 cups cubed, skinless roast (rotisserie) chicken meat	480 ml
½ cup thickened (whipping) cream	120 ml

- In large saucepan with boiling water, cook noodles according to package directions, and add snap peas to noodles 1 minute before noodles are done. Drain and return to saucepan.
- Add chicken stock (broth), lemon peel, chicken pieces and ½ teaspoon (2 ml) each of salt and pepper. Heat, stirring constantly, until thoroughly hot.
- Over low heat, gently stir in cream. Serve hot.

Sweet-and-Sour Chicken

6–8 boneless, skinless chicken breast halves	
Oil	
1 (1 ounce) packet dry onion soup mix	30 g
6 ounce orange juice cordial (concentrate)	180 ml

- Preheat oven to 180° C (350° F).
- Brown chicken in a little oil or butter and place in sprayed 23 x 33-cm (9 x 13-inch) baking dish.
- In small bowl, combine soup mix, orange cordial (concentrate)and ⅔ cup (160 ml) water, mix well and pour over chicken.
- Bake uncovered for 45 to 50 minutes.

More statistical studies are finding that family meals play a significant role in childhood development. Children who eat with their families four or more nights per week are healthier, achieve better grades in school, score higher on aptitude tests and are less likely to have problems with drugs.

Stir-Fry Chicken Spaghetti

1 pound boneless, skinless chicken breast halves	.5 kg
1½ cups mushrooms, sliced	360 ml
1½ cups capsicum (pepper) strips	360 ml
1 cup sweet-and-sour stir-fry sauce	240 ml
1 (16 ounce) package cooked spaghetti	.5 kg
¼ cup butter	60 ml

- Season chicken with a little salt and pepper and cut into thin slices. Brown chicken slices in large frying pan (skillet) with a little oil and cook for 5 minutes on medium-low heat. Transfer to plate and set aside.
- In same pan with a little more oil, stir-fry mushrooms and capsicum (pepper) strips for 5 minutes. Add chicken strips and sweet-and-sour sauce and stir until ingredients are hot.
- While spaghetti is still hot, drain well, add butter and stir until butter melts. Place in large bowl and toss with chicken mixture. Serve hot.

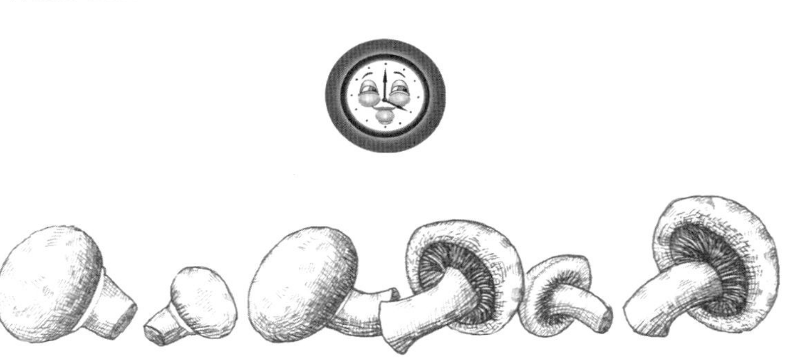

Hawaiian Chicken

2 small whole chickens, quartered	
Flour	
Oil	
1 (20 ounce) can sliced pineapple with juice	565 g
2 capsicums (peppers), cut in strips	

- Wash chicken and pat dry with paper towels.
- Coat chicken with a little salt and pepper and flour, brown in oil and place in shallow pan. Drain pineapple into 2-cup (480 ml) measure, add enough water (or orange juice) to make 1½ cups (360 ml) liquid and set aside.

Sauce for Hawaiian Chicken:

1 cup sugar	240 ml
3 tablespoons cornflour (cornstarch)	45 ml
¾ cup vinegar	180 ml
1 tablespoon lemon juice	15 ml
1 tablespoon soy sauce	15 ml
2 teaspoons chicken stock (bouillon) powder	10 ml

- Preheat oven to 180° C (350° F). In medium saucepan, combine reserved 1½ cups (360 ml) juice with sauce ingredients.
- Bring to a boil and stir constantly until thick and clear, then pour over chicken. Bake covered 40 minutes.
- Place pineapple and capsicum (pepper) on top of chicken and bake additional 10 minutes. Serve on white rice.

Green Chilli Chicken

5 boneless, skinless chicken breast halves	
1 (1 ounce) package hot-and-spicy coating mixture	30 g
1 (4 ounce) jar chopped green chillies	115 g
Chunky salsa	

- Preheat oven to 190° C (375° F).
- Dredge chicken in coating mixture and place in sprayed 23 x 33-cm (9 x 13-inch) baking dish.
- Bake for 25 minutes. Remove from oven, spread green chillies over chicken breasts and return to oven for 5 minutes. Serve with salsa over each chicken breast.

Apricot Chicken

1 cup apricot jam	240 ml
1 (8 ounce) bottle Thousand Island (catalina) salad dressing	225 g
1 (1 ounce) packet dry onion soup mix	30 g
6–8 boneless, skinless chicken breast halves	

- Preheat oven to 160° C (325° F).
- Combine apricot jam, salad dressing and soup mix. Place chicken breasts in large, sprayed baking dish and pour apricot mixture over chicken.
- Bake uncovered for 1 hour 20 minutes. Serve over rice.

Thousand Island Chicken

6–8 boneless, skinless chicken breast halves
1 (8 ounce) bottle Thousand Island (catalina) salad dressing — 225 g
1½ cups crushed biscuit (cracker) crumbs — 360 ml

- Preheat oven to 180° C (350° F).
- Marinate chicken breasts in dressing for 3 to 4 hours and discard marinade. Combine 1 teaspoon (5 ml) pepper and biscuit (cracker) crumbs.
- Dip each chicken breast in crumb mixture and place in large, sprayed baking dish. Bake uncovered for 1 hour.

Crispy Nutty Chicken

⅓ cup dry-roasted peanuts, minced — 80 ml
1 cup cornflake crumbs — 240 ml
½ cup ranch-style salad dressing — 120 ml
6 boneless, skinless chicken breast halves

- Preheat oven to 180° C (350° F).
- Combine peanuts and crumbs on wax paper.
- Pour dressing into shallow bowl, dip each piece of chicken in dressing and roll in crumb mixture to coat.
- Arrange chicken in shallow 23 x 33-cm (9 x 13-inch) baking dish. Bake uncovered for 50 minutes or until light brown.

One-Dish Chicken Bake

1 (1 ounce) packet dry vegetable soup mix	30 g
1 (6 ounce) package chicken stuffing mix	170 g
4 boneless, skinless chicken breast halves	
1 (10 ounce) can cream of mushroom soup	280 g
⅓ cup sour cream	80 ml

- Preheat oven to 190° C (375° F).
- Combine soup mix, stuffing mix and 1⅔ cups (400 ml) water and set aside.
- Place chicken in sprayed 23 x 33-cm (9 x 13-inch) baking dish.
- Mix and heat soup and sour cream in saucepan over low heat. Pour over chicken and spoon stuffing mixture evenly over top.
- Bake uncovered for 40 minutes.

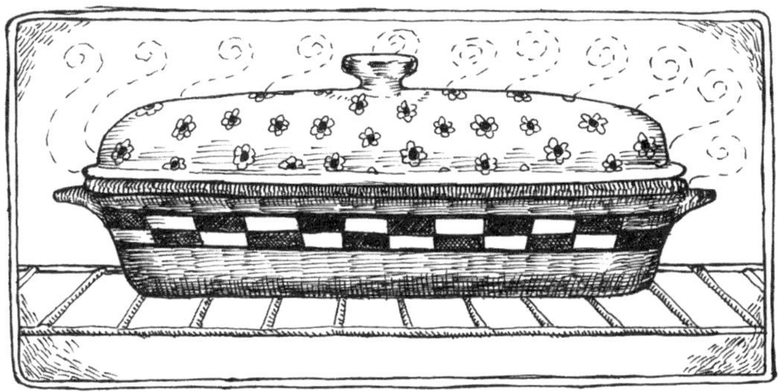

Favourite Chicken Breasts

6–8 boneless, skinless chicken breast halves	
1 (10 ounce) can mushroom soup	280 g
1 cup white wine or white cooking wine	240 ml
1 (8 ounce) carton sour cream	225 g

- Place chicken breasts in large, shallow baking pan, sprinkle with a little salt and pepper and bake uncovered at 180° C (350° F) for 30 minutes.
- In saucepan, combine soup, wine and sour cream and heat just enough to mix well.
- Remove chicken from oven and cover with soup mixture.
- Reduce heat to 150° C (300° F) and return to oven for additional 30 minutes. Baste twice.
- Serve over rice.

Chicken Bake

8 boneless, skinless chicken breast halves
8 slices Swiss cheese
1 (10 ounce) can cream of chicken soup **280 g**
1 (8 ounce) box chicken stuffing mix **225 g**

- Preheat oven to 160° C (325° F).
- Flatten each chicken breast with rolling pin and place in sprayed 23 x 33-cm (9 x 13-inch) baking dish.
- Place cheese slices over chicken.
- Combine chicken soup and ½ cup (120 ml) water and pour over chicken.
- Prepare stuffing mix according to package directions and sprinkle over chicken.
- Bake uncovered for 1 hour.

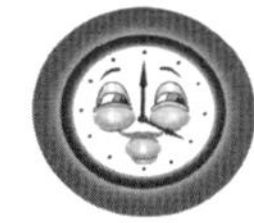

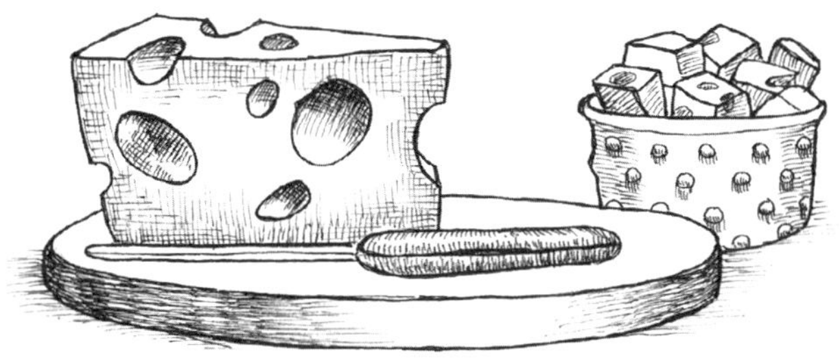

Mozzarella Cutlets

4 boneless, skinless chicken breast halves
1 cup dry seasoned breadcrumbs 240 ml
1 cup prepared spaghetti sauce 240 ml
4 slices mozzarella cheese

- Preheat oven to 180° C (350° F).
- Pound each chicken breast to flatten slightly.
- Coat chicken well in breadcrumbs and arrange in sprayed 23 x 33-cm (9 x 13-inch) baking dish.
- Spread a quarter of sauce over each portion.
- Place 1 slice cheese over each and garnish with remaining breadcrumbs.
- Bake uncovered for 45 minutes.

It is best to marinate whole chickens overnight. Boneless breast halves take up to 3 hours to reach full flavour.

Jiffy Chicken

8 boneless, skinless chicken breast halves

¾ cup mayonnaise	**180 ml**
2 cups crushed cornflakes	**480 ml**
½ cup parmesan cheese, grated	**120 ml**

- Preheat oven to 160° C (325° F).
- Sprinkle chicken breasts with a little salt and pepper.
- Dip chicken in mayonnaise and spread over chicken with brush.
- Combine cornflake crumbs and cheese and dip chicken in cornflake mixture until it coats completely.
- Place chicken in sprayed 23 x 33-cm (9 x 13-inch) glass baking dish and bake uncovered for 1 hour.

Look for baking dishes with lids. Any leftovers can be refrigerated right in the pan they were baked in and clean-up is a snap!

Honey-Baked Chicken

2 whole chickens, quartered	
½ cup butter, melted	120 ml
⅔ cup honey	160 ml
¼ cup Dijon mustard	60 ml
1 teaspoon curry powder	5 ml

- Preheat oven to 180° C (350° F).
- Place chicken pieces skin side up in large, shallow baking dish and sprinkle with a little salt.
- Combine butter, honey, mustard and curry powder and pour over chicken.
- Bake uncovered for 1 hour 5 minutes and baste every 20 minutes.

Party Chicken Breasts

6–8 boneless, skinless chicken breast halves
8 strips bacon
1 (2.5 ounce) jar beef jerky (dried beef) — 70 g
1 (10 ounce) can cream of chicken soup — 280 g
1 (8 ounce) carton sour cream — 225 g

- Preheat oven to 160° C (325° F).
- Wrap each chicken breast with 1 strip bacon and secure with toothpicks.
- Place beef jerky (dried beef) in bottom of large, shallow baking pan and place chicken on top.
- Heat soup and sour cream just enough to pour over chicken.
- Cover chicken with soup mixture and bake uncovered for 1 hour.

Always cook with thicker slices of bacon. Thin strips will fall apart when stretched around a chicken breast half. Don't forget to tell your guests that you used toothpicks to secure the meat.

Bacon-Wrapped Chicken

6 boneless, skinless chicken breast halves
1 (8 ounce) carton cream cheese with onion and chives 225 g
Butter
6 bacon strips

- Preheat oven to 190° C (375° F).
- Flatten chicken to 1-cm (½-inch) thickness and spread 3 tablespoons (45 ml) cream cheese over each piece.
- Dot with butter and sprinkle with a little salt, roll and wrap each with 1 bacon strip.
- Place seam-side down in sprayed 23 x 33-cm (9 x 13-inch) baking dish. Bake uncovered for 40 to 45 minutes or until juices run clear.
- To brown, grill (broil) 15 cm (6 inches) from heat for about 3 minutes or until bacon is crisp.

Broccoli-Cheese Chicken

4 boneless, skinless chicken breast halves	
1 tablespoon butter	15 ml
1 (10 ounce) jar processed cheese spread	280 g
1 (10 ounce) package frozen broccoli spears	280 g
⅓ cup milk	80 ml
½ cup water	120 ml

- In frying pan (skillet), cook chicken in butter for 15 minutes or until brown on both sides, remove and set aside.
- In same pan, combine soup, broccoli, milk, water and a little black pepper and heat to boiling. Return chicken to pan and reduce heat to low.
- Cover and cook additional 25 minutes or until chicken is no longer pink and broccoli is tender. Serve over rice.

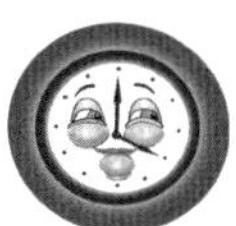

Asparagus-Cheese Chicken

1 tablespoon butter	**15 ml**
4 boneless, skinless chicken breast halves	
1 (10 ounce) jar processed cheese spread	**280 g**
1 (10 ounce) package frozen asparagus cuts	**280 g**
⅓ cup milk	**80 ml**
½ cup water	**120 ml**

- In frying pan (skillet), heat butter and cook chicken for 10 to 15 minutes or until brown on both sides.
- Remove chicken and set aside.
- In same pan, combine soup, asparagus, milk and water and heat to a boil.
- Return chicken to pan, reduce heat to low, cover and cook additional 25 minutes until chicken is no longer pink and asparagus is tender.

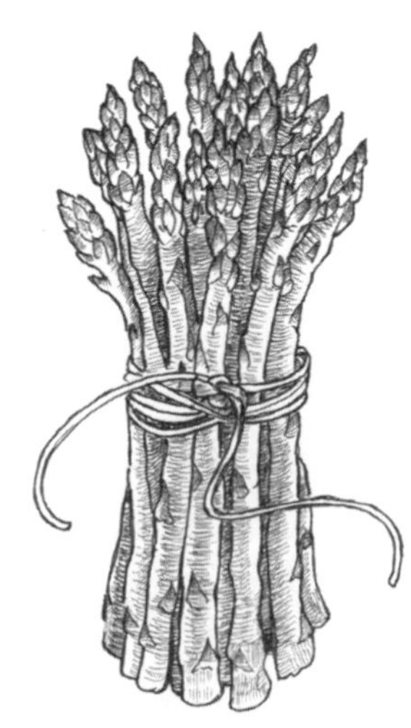

Cheesy Chicken and Potatoes

1 (20 ounce) package hash browns, shredded	570 g
½ cup green capsicum (pepper), chopped	120 ml
½ cup onion, chopped	120 ml
1 tablespoon minced garlic	15 ml
2–2½ cups bite-size chunks rotisserie chicken	480 ml
1 bunch spring (green) onions, sliced	
1 cup cheddar cheese, shredded	240 ml

- Add a little oil to large frying pan (skillet) over medium-high heat. Cook potatoes, capsicum (pepper) and onion for 7 minutes and turn frequently.
- Add garlic, chicken, spring (green) onions and ⅓ cup (80 ml) water and cook 5 to 6 minutes. Remove from heat and stir in cheese. Serve immediately right from pan.

Turkey Chilli

3 pounds turkey mince (ground turkey)	1.3 kg
½ teaspoon garlic powder	2 ml
3 tablespoons chilli powder	45 ml
1 (8 ounce) can tomato pasta sauce	225 g
Shredded cheese	

- In large saucepan, add turkey and garlic powder with 1 cup (240 ml) water. Cook over medium heat until mixture begins to fry.
- Add chilli powder and pasta sauce and simmer until meat is tender. Garnish with cheese.

PORK

Pineapple-Pork Chops

6–8 thick, boneless pork chops
1 cup pineapple juice 240 ml
3 tablespoons brown sugar 45 ml
⅓ cup wine or tarragon vinegar 80 ml
⅓ cup honey 80 ml

- Preheat oven to 160° C (325° F). Brown pork chops in a little oil in frying pan (skillet). Remove to shallow baking dish.
- Combine remaining ingredients and pour over chops. Cook covered for about 50 minutes. Serve over hot rice.

Oven-Pork Chops

6–8 medium-thick pork chops
1 (10 ounce) can cream of chicken soup 280 g
3 tablespoons tomato sauce (ketchup) 45 ml
1 tablespoon Worcestershire sauce 15 ml
1 medium onion, chopped

- Preheat oven to 180° C (350° F). Brown pork chops in a little oil and season with salt and pepper. Drain and place in shallow baking dish.
- Combine soup, tomato sauce (ketchup), Worcestershire and onion in small saucepan. Heat tomato sauce and pour over pork.
- Bake covered for 50 minutes. Uncover last 15 minutes.

Orange Pork Chops

6 (½ inch) thick boneless pork chops	**6 (1 cm)**
2 tablespoons oil	**30 ml**
1⅓ cups instant rice	**320 ml**
1 cup orange juice	**240 ml**
¼ teaspoon ground ginger	**1 ml**
1 (10 ounce) can condensed chicken soup	**280 g**
½ cup walnuts, chopped	**120 ml**

- Preheat oven to 180° C (350° F).
- Sprinkle a little salt and pepper over pork chops and brown in frying pan (skillet) with oil.
- Sprinkle rice into sprayed 18 x 28-cm (7 x 11-inch) baking dish. Add orange juice and arrange pork chops over rice.
- Add ginger to soup in can and stir. Pour soup over pork chops.
- Sprinkle walnuts over tops of pork chops.
- Cover and bake for 25 minutes.
- Uncover and bake additional 10 minutes or until rice is tender.

Spicy Pork Chops

4–6 pork chops	
1 large onion	
1 capsicum (pepper)	
1 (10 ounce) can diced tomatoes	**280 g**
1 (2 ounce) jar green chillies	**55 g**

- Preheat oven to 180° C (350° F).
- Brown pork chops in frying pan (skillet) with a little oil.
- Spray baking dish and place chops in dish.
- Cut onion and capsicum (pepper) into large chunks and place on chops.
- Pour tomatoes and green chillies over chops and sprinkle with 1 teaspoon (5 ml) salt.
- Bake covered for 45 minutes.

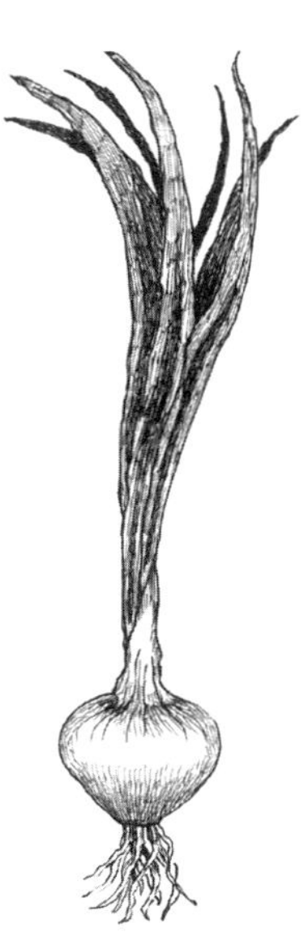

Pork Chops in Cream Gravy

4 (¼ inch) thick pork chops 4 (.5 cm)
Flour
Oil
2¼ cups milk 540 ml

- Trim all fat off pork chops. Dip chops in flour with a little salt and pepper. Brown pork chops on both sides in a little oil. Remove chops from frying pan (skillet).
- Add about 2 tablespoons (30 ml) flour to pan, brown lightly and stir in a little salt and pepper. Slowly stir in milk to make gravy.
- Return chops to pan with gravy. Cover and simmer on low burner for about 40 minutes. Serve over rice.

Pork Casserole

4–5 potatoes, peeled, sliced
6 pork chops
1 (10 ounce) box processed cheese spread with chopped jalapeño chillies 280 g
5 ounce milk 150 ml

- Preheat oven to 180° C (350° F). Place 2 layers potatoes in sprayed baking dish and place pork chops on top.
- Combine cheese, jalapeños and milk and heat just enough to pour over chops. Bake covered for 45 minutes. Uncover and bake additional 15 minutes.

Pork Chops and Apples

Simple and delicious!

6 thick-cut pork chops
Flour
Oil
3 baking apples

- Preheat oven to 160° C (325° F).
- Dip pork chops in flour and coat well.
- In frying pan (skillet), brown pork chops in oil and place in sprayed 23 x 33-cm (9 x 13-inch) baking dish.
- Add ⅓ cup (80 ml) water to casserole and bake covered for 50 minutes.
- Peel, halve and seed apples and place half an apple over each pork chop.
- Return to oven for 10 minutes. (Don't overcook apples.)

Oven Pork Chops

6–8 medium-thick pork chops	
1 (10 ounce) can cream of chicken soup	280 g
3 tablespoons tomato sauce (ketchup)	45 ml
1 tablespoon Worcestershire sauce	15 ml
1 medium onion, chopped	

- Preheat oven to 180° C (350° F).
- Brown pork chops in a little oil, season with a little salt and pepper and place drained pork chops in shallow baking dish.
- In saucepan, combine soup, tomato sauce (ketchup), Worcestershire and onion, heat just enough to mix and pour over pork chops.
- Bake covered for 50 minutes. Uncover for the last 15 minutes of baking time.

Tangy Pork Chops

4–6 pork chops	
¼ cup Worcestershire sauce	60 ml
¼ cup tomato sauce (ketchup)	60 ml
½ cup honey	120 ml

- Preheat oven to 160° C (325° F). In frying pan (skillet), brown pork chops and remove to shallow baking dish.
- Combine Worcestershire, tomato sauce (ketchup) and honey. Pour over pork chops. Cover and bake for 45 minutes.

Onion-Smothered Pork Chops

6 (½ inch) thick pork chops	6 (1 cm)
1 tablespoon oil	15 ml
2 tablespoons butter	30 ml
1 onion, chopped	
1 (10 ounce) can French onion soup	280 g

- Preheat oven to 160° C (325° F).
- In frying pan (skillet), brown pork chops in oil, simmer about 10 minutes and place pork chops in sprayed shallow baking dish.
- In same frying pan, add butter and saute chopped onion. (Pan juices are brown from pork chops so onions will be brown from juices already in pan.)
- Add onion soup and ½ cup (120 ml) water and stir well. (Sauce will have a nice, light brown colour.)
- Pour onion mixture over pork chops. Cover and bake for 40 minutes and serve over brown rice.

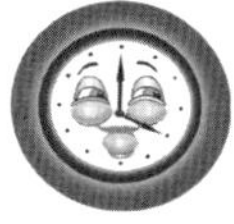

Peachy Glazed Ham

1 (15 ounce) can sliced peaches in light syrup with juice	425 g
2 tablespoons brown sugar	30 ml
2 teaspoons Dijon mustard	10 ml
1 pound centre-cut ham slice	.5 kg
⅓ cup spring (green) onions, sliced	80 ml

- Drain peaches, reserve ½ cup (120 ml) juice in large frying pan (skillet) and set peaches aside.
- Add brown sugar and mustard to pan, bring to a boil over medium-high heat and cook 2 minutes or until slightly reduced.
- Add ham and cook 2 minutes on each side.
- Add peaches and onions, cover and cook over low heat for 3 minutes or until peaches are thoroughly hot.

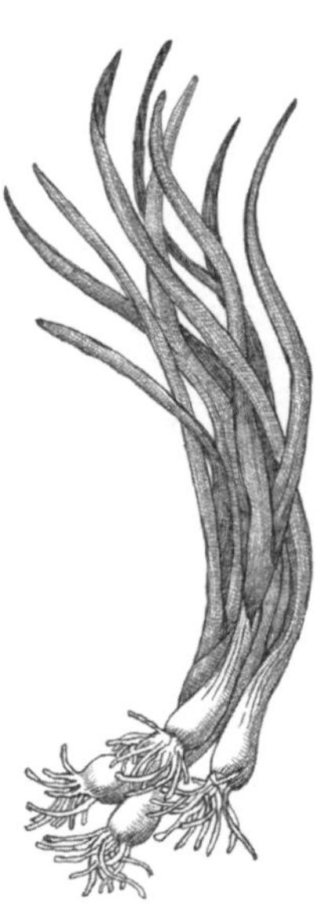

Baked Ham and Pineapple

1 (6–8 pound) fully cooked, bone-in ham	2.7 kg
Whole cloves	
½ cup brown sugar	120 ml
1 (8 ounce) can sliced pineapple with juice	225 g
5 glacé (maraschino) cherries	

- Preheat oven to 160° C (325° F).
- Place ham in roasting pan, score surface with shallow diagonal cuts (to make diamond shapes) and insert cloves into diamonds.
- Cover and bake for 1 hour 30 minutes.
- Combine brown sugar and juice from pineapple and pour over ham.
- Arrange pineapple slices and cherries on ham. Bake, uncovered, additional 40 minutes.

Praline Ham

2 (½ inch) thick ham slices, cooked (about 2½ pounds)	2 (1 cm)/1.2 kg
½ cup maple syrup	120 ml
3 tablespoons brown sugar	45 ml
1 tablespoon butter	15 ml
⅓ cup pecans, chopped	80 ml

- Heat ham slices in shallow pan at 160° C (325° F) for 10 minutes.
- Bring syrup, sugar and butter to a boil in small saucepan and stir often. Stir in pecans and spoon syrup mixture over ham. Warm additional 20 minutes.

Sausage Casserole

1 pound pork sausage	.5 kg
2 (15 ounce) cans baked beans with ham	2 (425 g)
1 (15 ounce) can tomatoes with chopped fresh coriander (cilantro) and lime juice added (to taste)	425 g
8 ounce prepared polenta (cornmeal) muffin mix	230 g

- Preheat oven to 200° C (400° F).
- Brown sausage and drain fat. Add beans and tomatoes, mix through and bring to a boil. Pour mixture into sprayed 3-L (3-quart) baking dish.
- Drop muffin mix by teaspoonfuls over meat-bean mixture. Bake for 30 minutes or until top browns.

Apricot-Baked Ham

1 (12–20 pound) whole ham, fully cooked	5–8.5 kg
Whole cloves	
2 tablespoons dry mustard	30 ml
1¼ cups apricot jam	300 ml
1¼ cups light brown sugar	300 ml

- Preheat oven to 230° C (450° F).
- Place ham on rack in large roasting pan and insert cloves into ham every 2 cm (1 inch) or so.
- Combine dry mustard and jam and spread over entire surface of ham.
- Pat brown sugar over jam mixture. Reduce heat to 160° C (325° F) and bake uncovered for 15 minutes per 2 kg (1 pound).

The best way to avoid freezer burn is to wrap food twice in plastic wrap and seal in an air-tight plastic bag. Be sure to date your package and label it with a permanent marker.

Walnut-Ham Linguine

2 teaspoons minced garlic	**10 ml**
½ cup walnuts, coarsely chopped	**120 ml**
1 red capsicum (pepper), thinly sliced	
¼ cup olive oil	**60 ml**
½ pound cooked ham, cut in strips	**225 g**
1 (16 ounce) jar creamy alfredo sauce	**.5 kg**
¼ cup parmesan cheese, grated	**60 ml**
1 (12 ounce) package linguine, cooked al dente	**340 g**
1 cup seasoned breadcrumbs	**240 ml**

- Preheat oven to 180° C (350° F).
- In large frying pan (skillet), saute garlic, walnuts and capsicum (pepper) in oil for 1 to 2 minutes.
- In large bowl, combine garlic-capsicum mixture, ham, alfredo sauce, parmesan cheese and linguine and mix well.
- Spoon into sprayed 3-L (3-quart) baking dish. Sprinkle breadcrumbs over top.
- Bake uncovered for 35 minutes or until breadcrumbs are light brown.

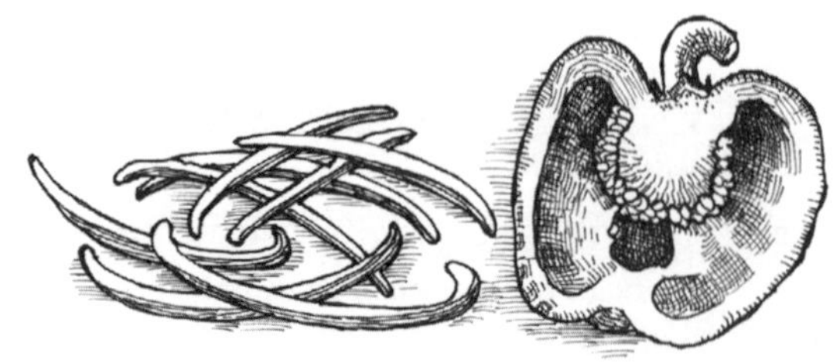

Sandwich Souffle

A fun lunch!

Butter, softened
8 slices white bread, crusts removed
4 slices ham
4 slices cheddar (American) cheese
2 cups milk **480 ml**
2 eggs, beaten

- Preheat oven to 190° C (375° F).
- Butter bread on both sides, make 4 sandwiches with ham and cheese.
- Place sandwiches in sprayed 20-cm (8-inch) square baking pan. Beat milk, eggs and a little salt and pepper. Pour over sandwiches and soak for 1 to 2 hours. Bake for 45 to 50 minutes.

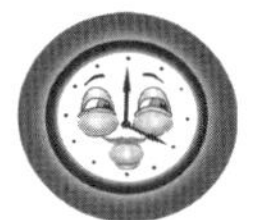

Grilled Pork Loin

1 (4 pound) boneless pork loin roast (rotisserie)	1.8 kg
1 (8 ounce) bottle Italian salad dressing	240 ml
1 cup dry white wine	240 ml
3 cloves garlic, minced	
10 black peppercorns	

- Pierce roast at 2.5-cm (1-inch) intervals with fork and set aside.
- Combine salad dressing, white wine, garlic and peppercorns. Reserve ½ cup (120 ml) mixture for basting during cooking.
- Place roast in large, resealable plastic bag with remaining mixture, chill 8 hours and turn occasionally.
- Remove roast from marinade and discard marinade.
- Place roast on rack in barbeque (or broiler).
- Cook, covered with barbeque lid, for 35 minutes or until meat thermometer inserted into thickest portion reaches 70° C (160° F). Turn occasionally and baste with ½ cup (120 ml) reserved dressing mixture.

Ham and Potatoes Olé!

1 (24 ounce) package hash browns, shredded	680 g
½ cup capsicum (pepper), chopped	120 ml
½ cup onion, chopped	120 ml
3 cups cooked ham, cubed	710 ml
1 (10 ounce) can cream of chicken soup	280 g
1 (10 ounce) jar processed cheese spread	280 g
1 cup hot salsa	240 ml
8 ounce cheddar cheese, shredded	225 g

- Preheat oven to 180° C (350° F). Combine potatoes, ham, soup, cheese spread and salsa in large bowl and mix well.
- Spoon into sprayed 23 x 33-cm (9 x 13-inch) baking dish. Cover and cook for 40 minutes. Remove from oven, sprinkle cheese over casserole and bake uncovered additional 5 minutes.

Pineapple Sauce for Ham

Pre-sliced, cooked honey-baked ham slices	
1 (15 ounce) can pineapple pieces (tidbits) with juice	425 g
1 cup apricot jam (jelly)	240 ml
1¼ cups brown sugar	300 ml
¼ teaspoon cinnamon	1 ml

- Place ham slices in shallow baking pan. In saucepan, combine pineapple, apricot jam (jelly), brown sugar and cinnamon and heat. Pour sauce over ham slices and heat.

Lemon Spare Ribs

4 pounds pork spare ribs	1.8 kg
6 ounces lemon juice cordial (concentrate)	180 ml
½ teaspoon garlic salt	2 ml
⅓ cup soy sauce	80 ml

- Preheat oven to 180° C (350° F).
- Place ribs, meaty-side down, in shallow roasting pan and cook covered for 40 minutes.
- Remove cover, drain fat and return ribs to oven.
- Bake additional 30 minutes and drain fat again.
- Combine lemon cordial (concentrate), garlic salt and soy sauce and brush on ribs.
- Reduce temperature to 160° C (325° F), cover and bake for additional 1 hour or until ribs are tender. Brush occasionally with sauce.

Moroccan Baby-Back Ribs

4 pounds baby-back pork ribs	1.8 kg
1 (12 ounce) bottle Moroccan marinade, divided	340 g

- Cut ribs in lengths to fit in large, sealable plastic bag.
- Place ribs, ¾ cup (180 ml) marinade and a little pepper in bag and shake to coat. Refrigerate overnight. Place ribs in sprayed shallow baking dish and discard used marinade.
- Cover ribs with foil and bake at 190° C (375° F) for 30 minutes. Remove from oven and spread remaining marinade over ribs.
- Reduce heat to 150° C (300° F) and cook 1 hour. Uncover to let ribs brown and bake additional 30 minutes.

Hawaiian Pork

This is great served over rice.

2 pound lean pork tenderloin, cut into 1-inch cubes	1 kg/2.5 cm
1 (15 ounce) can pineapple pieces (tidbits) with juice	425 g
1 (12 ounce) bottle chilli sauce	340 g
1 teaspoon ground ginger	5 ml

- In frying pan (skillet), season pork with a little salt and pepper. Combine meat, pineapple with juice, chilli sauce and ginger. Simmer covered for 1 hour 30 minutes.

Sweet-and-Sour Spare Ribs

3–4 pounds spare ribs	1.3–2 kg
3 tablespoons soy sauce	45 ml
⅓ cup mustard	80 ml
1 cup brown sugar	240 ml
½ teaspoon garlic salt	2 ml

- Place spare ribs in roasting pan, bake at 160° C (325° F) for 45 minutes and drain.
- Make sauce with soy sauce, mustard, brown sugar and garlic salt and brush on ribs.
- Return to oven, reduce heat to 150° C (300° F) and bake for 2 hours or until ribs are tender. Baste several times.

Tenderloin with Apricot Sauce

3 pound pork tenderloin	1.3 kg
1 cup apricot jam (jelly)	240 ml
⅓ cup lemon juice	80 ml
⅓ cup tomato sauce (ketchup)	80 ml
1 tablespoon soy sauce	15 ml

- Preheat oven to 160° C (325° F). Place tenderloins in roasting pan. Combine jam (jelly), lemon juice, tomato sauce (ketchup) and soy sauce.
- Pour jam mixture over pork and bake covered for 1 hour 20 minutes. Baste once. Serve over rice.

One-Dish Pork and Peas

This blend of ingredients makes a delicious dish.

2 pound pork tenderloin	1 kg
2 tablespoons oil, divided	30 ml
1½ cups celery, sliced	360 ml
1 large onion, chopped	
2 red capsicum (peppers), seeded, chopped	
1 (12 ounce) package small egg noodles, cooked, drained	340 g
1 (10 ounce) can cream of chicken soup	280 g
10 ounce chicken liquid stock (broth)	300 ml
1 (8 ounce) carton thickened (whipping) cream	225 g
1 (10 ounce) package frozen green peas, thawed	280 g
1½ teaspoons seasoned salt	7 ml
1 teaspoon black pepper	5 ml
1½ cups seasoned dry breadcrumbs	360 ml
¾ cup walnuts, chopped	180 ml

- Preheat oven to 180° C (350° F).
- Cut pork tenderloin into 1-cm (½-inch) cubes. In large frying pan (skillet), brown pork in 1 tablespoon (15 ml) oil. Reduce heat and cook 25 minutes. Remove pork to separate dish. In a little oil, saute celery, onion and capsicum (pepper).
- Add pork, noodles, soup, stock (broth), cream, peas, salt and pepper; mix well. Spoon into sprayed 25 x 38-cm (10 x 15-inch) baking dish. Sprinkle with breadcrumbs and walnuts.
- Bake uncovered for 35 to 45 minutes or until bubbly around edges and breadcrumbs are light brown. Serves 20.

SEAFOOD

Crispy Fish and Cheese Fillets

2 pounds fish fillets	1 kg
½ cup ranch-style salad dressing	120 ml
1½ cups cheese biscuits (crackers), crushed	360 ml
2 tablespoons butter, melted	30 ml

- Preheat oven to 220° C (425° F).
- Cut fish into serving portions, dip into dressing and roll in cracker crumbs.
- Place in sprayed shallow pan and drizzle butter over fish.
- Bake uncovered for 15 minutes or until fish flakes easily.

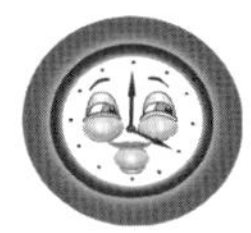

There is usually a thin end on most fish fillets. When cooking fillets, fold thin end over fillet until it is about the same thickness as the thicker end.

Baked Fish

1 pound fish fillets	.5 kg
3 tablespoons butter	45 ml
1 teaspoon dried tarragon	5 ml
2 teaspoons capers	10 ml
2 tablespoons lemon juice	30 ml

- Preheat oven to 190° C (375° F).
- Place fish fillets and a little butter in sprayed shallow pan and sprinkle with a little salt and pepper.
- Bake for about 15 to 16 minutes, turn and bake additional 4 to 6 minutes or until fish flakes.
- For sauce, melt 3 tablespoons (45 ml) butter with tarragon, capers and lemon juice and serve over warm fish.

Chips and Fish

3–4 fish fillets, rinsed, dried
1 cup mayonnaise 240 ml
2 tablespoons fresh lime juice and lime wedges 30 ml
1½ cups corn (tortilla) chips, crushed 360 ml

- Preheat oven to 220° C (425° F).
- Mix mayonnaise and lime juice and spread on both sides of fish fillets.
- Place crushed corn (tortilla) chips on wax paper, dredge both sides of fish in chips and shake off excess chips.
- Place fillets on foil-covered baking tray (sheet) and bake for 15 minutes or until fish flakes.
- Serve with lime wedges.

Golden Snapper Fillets

3 eggs	
¾ cup plain (all-purpose) flour	180 ml
¾ cup polenta (cornmeal)	180 ml
1 teaspoon garlic powder	5 ml
6–8 (4–8 ounce) snapper fillets	6–8 (115 g)

- In shallow bowl, beat eggs until foamy.
- In another shallow bowl, combine flour, polenta (cornmeal), garlic powder and a little salt.
- Dip fillets in eggs and coat with polenta mixture.
- Heat .5 cm (¼ inch) oil in large frying pan and fry fish over medium-high heat for about 4 minutes on each side or until fish flakes easily with fork.

Fish like salmon, tuna and mackerel are considered fatty fish, but are still healthy and nutritional. It is thought that fish help to prevent heart disease and even aid in preventing other illnesses like Alzheimer's disease and strokes.

Flounder au Gratin

½ cup fine dry breadcrumbs	120 ml
¼ cup parmesan cheese, grated	60 ml
1 pound flounder fillets	.5 kg
⅓ cup mayonnaise	80 ml

- Preheat oven to 190° C (375° F).
- In shallow dish, combine breadcrumbs and cheese.
- Brush both sides of fish with mayonnaise and coat with crumb mixture.
- Arrange fillets in single layer in shallow pan and bake for 20 to 25 minutes or until fish flakes easily.

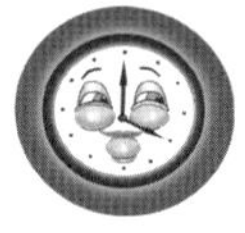

Flounder fillets will usually have the skin intact. In this case, look for skin with a glossy appearance. If the fish is whole, make sure the eye is clear, not foggy.

Lemon-Dill Fillets

½ cup mayonnaise	120 ml
2 tablespoons lemon juice	30 ml
½ teaspoon lemon zest	2 ml
1 teaspoon dill (dill weed)	5 ml
1 pound snapper or flounder fillets	.5 kg

- Combine mayonnaise, lemon juice, lemon zest and dill until they blend well.
- Place fish on sprayed grill (broiler) rack and brush with half mayonnaise mixture.
- Grill (broil) 5 to 8 minutes, turn and brush with remaining mayonnaise mixture.
- Continue grilling 5 to 8 minutes or until fish flakes easily with fork.

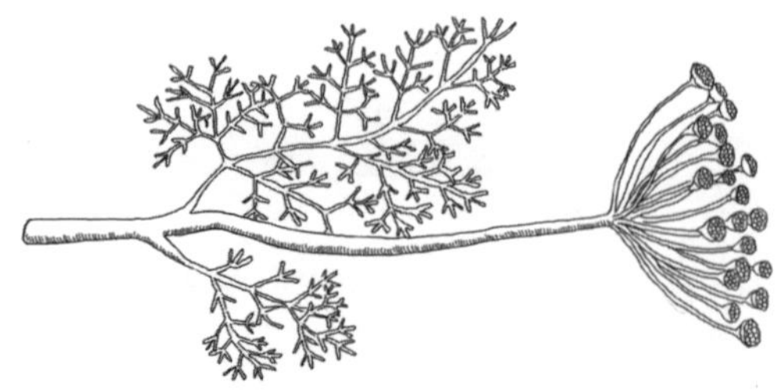

Lemon-Baked Fish

1 pound fish fillets	.5 kg
2 tablespoons butter	30 ml
1 teaspoon dried tarragon	5 ml
2 tablespoons lemon juice	30 ml

- Preheat oven to 190° C (375° F).
- Place fish fillets in sprayed shallow pan with a little butter and sprinkle with salt and pepper.
- Bake for 8 to 10 minutes, turn and bake additional 6 minutes or until fish flakes.
- Melt 2 tablespoons (30 ml) butter with tarragon and lemon juice and serve over warm fish fillets.

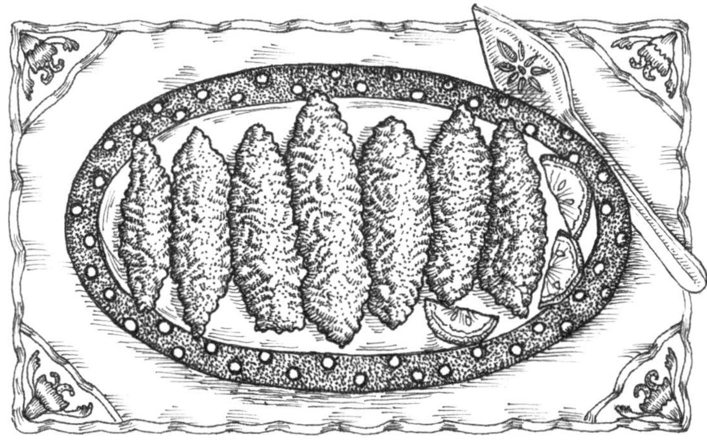

Baked Fish Steaks

2 (1 inch) thick white fish steaks	**2 (2.5 cm)**
1 (8 ounce) carton sour cream	**225 g**
½ cup parmesan cheese, grated	**120 ml**
¾ teaspoon dill (dill weed)	**4 ml**
Paprika	

- Preheat oven to 160° C (325° F).
- Place fish steaks in sprayed 23 x 33-cm (9 x 13-inch) baking dish.
- Combine sour cream, parmesan cheese and dill (and salt and pepper, if desired) and spoon over fish.
- Cover and bake for 20 minutes.
- Uncover and sprinkle with paprika.
- Bake additional 10 minutes or until fish flakes easily with fork.

The halibut is a relative of the flounder, albeit a much larger one. Halibut are found in cold waters and can weigh as much as 270 kg (600 pounds).

Hake with Herbs

1 pound hake fillets	.5 kg
1 onion, sliced	
2 red capsicum (peppers), cut into julienne strips	
1 teaspoon dried thyme leaves	5 ml

- Cut fish into 4 serving-size pieces.
- Heat a little oil in frying pan (skillet), layer onion and capsicum (peppers) in oil and sprinkle with half thyme and ¼ teaspoon pepper.
- Place fish over capsicum and sprinkle with remaining thyme.
- Turn burner on high just until fish begins to cook.
- Lower heat, cover and cook fish for 15 to 20 minutes or until fish flakes easily.

When buying a whole fish check to make sure the eyes are clear and the meat is firm. When buying fillets or steaks, be sure meat is uniform in colour with no brown spots.

Chipper Fish

2 pounds sole	1 kg
½ cup Caesar salad dressing	120 ml
1 cup potato chips, crushed	240 ml
½ cup cheddar cheese, shredded	120 ml

- Preheat oven to 190° C (375° F).
- Dip fish in dressing and place in sprayed baking dish.
- Combine potato chips and cheese and sprinkle over fish.
- Bake for about 20 to 25 minutes.

The most important thing to remember about cooking fish is not to overcook it. The internal temperature should be about 65° C (145° F) and the meat should be opaque. Don't let fish dry out.

Boiled Seafood

3 pounds fresh prawns (shrimp)	1.3 kg
2 teaspoons seafood seasoning	10 ml
½ cup vinegar	120 ml

- Remove heads from prawns (shrimp).
- Place all ingredients and 1 teaspoon (5 ml) salt in large saucepan, cover prawns with water and bring to a boil.
- Reduce heat and boil for 10 minutes.
- Remove from heat, drain and chill.

Beer-Batter Seafood

1 (12 ounce) can beer	350 ml
1 cup plain (all-purpose) flour	240 ml
2 teaspoons garlic powder	10 ml
1 pound prawns (shrimp), peeled, deveined	.5kg

- Combine beer, flour and garlic powder and stir to creamy consistency to make batter.
- Dip prawns (shrimp) into batter to cover and deep-fry in hot oil.

Seafood Delight

1 (6 ounce) can shrimp, drained **170 g**
1 (6 ounce) can crabmeat, drained, flaked **170 g**
1 (10 ounce) can creamed (cream-style) corn **280 g**
2–3 cups dry, seasoned breadcrumbs, divided **480 ml**

- Preheat oven to 180° C (350° F).
- Mix shrimp, crabmeat, corn and ⅓ cup (80 ml) breadcrumbs.
- Place mixture in sprayed 1.5-L (1½-quart) baking dish and sprinkle with remaining breadcrumbs.
- Bake for 30 minutes or until casserole bubbles and breadcrumbs are light brown.

Creamed Shrimp Over Rice

5 (6 ounce) cans shrimp, drained **5 (170 g)**
1 (1 pint) carton sour cream **.5 kg**
1 cup milk **240 ml**
1½ teaspoons curry powder **7 ml**

- Combine all ingredients in bain-marie (double boiler).
- Heat and stir constantly, but do not boil.
- Serve over hot, cooked rice.

Crabmeat Casserole

2 (6 ounce) cans crabmeat, drained, flaked	2 (170 g)
3 ounces fried onion rings	85 g
1 (10 ounce) can cream of chicken soup	280 g
¾ cup biscuit (cracker) crumbs	180 ml

- Preheat oven to 180° C (350° F).
- In bowl, combine crabmeat, half fried onions, soup and biscuit (cracker) crumbs and mix well.
- Place in sprayed baking dish and top with remaining onions. Bake covered for 30 minutes.

Tuna and Chips

1 (6 ounce) can tuna, drained	170 g
1 (10 ounce) can cream of chicken soup	280 g
¾ cup milk	180 ml
1½ cups potato chips, crushed, divided	360 ml

- Preheat oven to 180° C (350° F).
- Break chunks of tuna into bowl and stir in soup and milk. Add ¾ cup (180 ml) crushed potato chips and mix well.
- Pour mixture into sprayed baking dish and sprinkle remaining chips over top.
- Bake uncovered for 30 minutes or until chips are light brown.

Crab Mornay

2 (6 ounce) cans crabmeat, drained	2 (170 g)
1 cup cream of mushroom soup	240 ml
½ cup Swiss cheese, shredded	120 ml
½ cup seasoned breadcrumbs	120 ml

- Preheat oven to 180° C (350° F).
- Combine crabmeat, soup and cheese and mix well.
- Pour into sprayed 1.5-L (1½-quart) baking dish and sprinkle with breadcrumbs.
- Bake uncovered for 30 minutes or until soup bubbles and breadcrumbs are brown.

Baked Oysters

1 cup oysters, drained, rinsed	240 ml
2 cups biscuit (cracker) crumbs	480 ml
¼ cup butter, melted	60 ml
½ cup milk	120 ml

- Preheat oven to 180° C (350° F).
- Make alternating layers of oysters, biscuit (cracker) crumbs and butter in 18 x 28-cm (7 x 11-inch) baking dish.
- Pour warmed milk over layers and add lots of salt and pepper.
- Bake for 35 minutes.

Salmon Croquettes

1 (15 ounce) can pink salmon, drained, flaked	**425 g**
1 egg	
½ cup scone (biscuit) mix	**120 ml**
¼ cup tomato sauce (ketchup)	**60 ml**

- Combine salmon (discard skin and bones) and egg in bowl.
- Add scone (biscuit) mix and tomato sauce (ketchup) and mix well. Shape croquette into triangles about 8 cm (3 inches) long.
- Heat a little oil in frying pan (skillet) and place each croquette into pan.
- Cook each side until brown.

Before squeezing the juice from lemons, limes or oranges, scrape the outside rind (called zest) to get just the coloured part of the rind. Even if your recipe doesn't call for it, save it in airtight plastic bags for flavouring all kinds of dishes.

DESSERTS

Pecan-Topped Toffee

1 cup butter	**240 ml**
1¼ cups brown sugar	**300 ml**
6 (1.5 ounce) milk chocolate bars	**6 (45 g)**
⅔ cup pecans, finely chopped	**160 ml**

- In saucepan, combine butter and brown sugar and cook on medium-high heat.
- Stir constantly until mixture reaches 148° C (300° F) on cooking thermometer and pour immediately into sprayed 23-cm (9-inch) baking pan.
- Lay chocolate bars evenly over hot toffee.
- When chocolate is soft, spread into smooth layer.
- Sprinkle pecans over chocolate and press lightly with back of spoon.
- Chill in refrigerator for 1 hour.
- Invert toffee onto greaseproof (wax) paper and break into small, irregular pieces.

Microwave Pralines

1½ cups brown sugar	360 ml
⅔ cup unthickened (half-and-half) cream	160 ml
2 tablespoons butter, melted	30 ml
1⅔ cups pecans, chopped	400 ml

- Combine brown sugar, cream and dash of salt in deep glass dish and mix well. Blend in butter.
- Microwave on high for 10 minutes, stir once and add pecans. Cool for 1 minute.
- Beat by hand until creamy and thick, about 4 to 5 minutes. (The mixture will lose some of its gloss.)
- Drop by tablespoonfuls onto greaseproof (wax) paper.

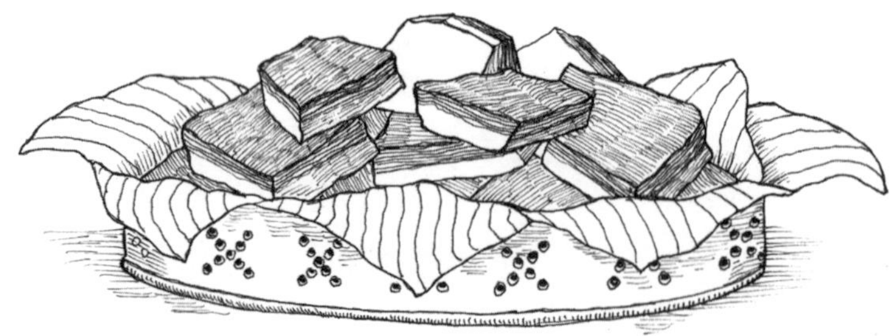

Dream Treats

16 ounce thickened (whipping) cream	475 ml
3 cups sugar	710 ml
1 cup light glucose (corn) syrup	240 ml
1 cup pecans, chopped	240 ml

- In saucepan, combine cream, sugar and syrup and cook to soft-ball stage (115° C/234° F on cooking thermometer).
- Stir and beat until mixture is cool. Add pecans and pour into sprayed 23-cm (9-inch) pan.

Caramel Crunch

½ cup firmly packed brown sugar	120 ml
½ cup light glucose (corn) syrup	120 ml
4 tablespoons butter	60 ml
6 cups bite-size crispy corn cereal squares	1.5 L
2 cups peanuts	480 ml

- In large saucepan, heat brown sugar, syrup and butter. Stir constantly until sugar and butter melt.
- Add cereal and peanuts and stir until all ingredients are well coated.
- Spread mixture on lightly sprayed baking tray (sheet) and bake at 120° C (250° F) for 30 minutes. Stir occasionally while baking.
- Cool and store in airtight container.

Peanut Brittle

2 cups sugar	480 ml
½ cup light glucose (corn) syrup	120 ml
2 cups dry-roasted peanuts	480 ml
1 tablespoon butter	15 ml
1 teaspoon bicarbonate of soda (baking soda)	5 ml

- Combine sugar and syrup in saucepan. Stir constantly over low heat until sugar dissolves. Cover and cook over medium heat another 2 minutes.
- Uncover, add peanuts and cook, stirring occasionally, to hard-crack stage 148° C (300° F). Stir in butter and bicarbonate of soda (baking soda), pour into sprayed rectangular pan and spread thinly. Cool and break into pieces.

White Chocolate Fudge

1 (8 ounce) package cream cheese, softened	225 g
4 cups icing (powdered) sugar	1 L
1½ teaspoons vanilla extract	7 ml
1 (12 ounce) package almond bark, melted	340 g
¾ cup pecans, chopped	180 ml

- Beat cream cheese at medium speed with mixer until smooth, gradually add sugar and vanilla and beat well. Stir in melted almond bark and pecans and spread into sprayed 20-cm (8-inch) square pan.
- Refrigerate until firm and cut into small squares.

Diamond Fudge

1 (6 ounce) package dark (semi-sweet) chocolate chips	170 g
1 cup smooth peanut butter	240 ml
½ cup butter	120 ml
1 cup icing (confectioner's) sugar	240 ml

- Combine chocolate chips, peanut butter and butter in saucepan over low heat. Stir constantly, just until mixture melts and is smooth.
- Remove from heat, add sugar and stir until smooth.
- Spoon into sprayed 20-cm (8-inch) square pan and chill until firm.
- Let stand 10 minutes at room temperature before cutting into squares, and store in refrigerator.

Microwave Fudge

3 cups dark (semi-sweet) chocolate chips	710 ml
1 (14 ounce) can sweetened condensed milk	395 g
¼ cup butter, sliced	60 ml
1 cup walnuts, chopped	240 ml

- Combine chocolate chips, sweetened condensed milk and butter in 2-L (2-quart) glass bowl.
- Microwave on medium for 4 to 5 minutes and stir at 1½-minute intervals.
- Stir in walnuts and pour into sprayed 20-cm (8-inch) square dish.
- Chill 2 hours and cut into squares.

Nutty Blonde Brownies

16 ounce brown sugar	.5 kg
4 eggs	
2 cups scone (biscuit) mix	480 ml
2 cups pecans, chopped	480 ml

- Preheat oven to 180° C (350° F).
- In mixing bowl, beat brown sugar, eggs and scone (biscuit) mix.
- Stir in pecans and pour into sprayed 23 x 33-cm (9 x 13-inch) baking pan. Bake for 35 minutes, cool and cut into squares.

Nutty Brownies

1 (18 ounce) box chocolate cake mix	510 g
¾ cup butter, melted	180 ml
½ cup evaporated milk	120 ml
4 (2.7 ounce) nut and caramel chocolate (candy) bars, cut in 3 mm (⅛-inch) slices	4 (70 g)

- Preheat oven to 180° C (350° F).
- In large bowl, combine cake mix, butter and evaporated milk and beat on low speed until mixture blends well.
- Place half batter in sprayed, floured 23 x 33-cm (9 x 13-inch) baking pan and bake for 10 minutes.
- Remove from oven and place chocolate (candy) bar slices evenly over brownies.
- Drop remaining half of batter by spoonfuls over chocolate bars and spread as evenly as possible.
- Return to oven and bake for additional 20 minutes. When cool, cut into bars.

Brownies are really easy to make and always a popular choice. About the only way you can really mess up brownies is to overcook them. Fudgy brownies are a little better if they are slightly undercooked. Cake brownies are best with icing.

Gooey Turtle Bars

½ cup butter, melted	120 ml
2 cups vanilla biscuit (wafer) crumbs	480 ml
12 ounce dark (semi-sweet) chocolate chips	340 g
1 cup pecan pieces	240 ml
1 (12 ounce) jar caramel topping	340 g

- Preheat oven to 180° C (350° F).
- Combine butter and biscuit (wafer) crumbs in 23 x 33-cm (9 x 13-inch) baking pan and press into bottom of pan. Sprinkle with chocolate chips and pecans.
- Remove lid from caramel topping and microwave on high for 30 seconds or until hot. Drizzle topping over pecans.
- Bake for about 15 minutes or until chocolate chips melt.
- Cool in pan and chill at least 30 minutes before cutting into squares.

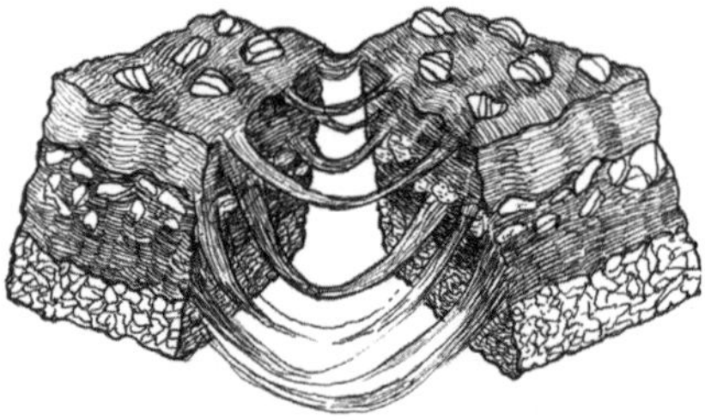

TIP: Watch bars closely – you want the chips to melt, but you don't want the crumbs to burn.

Apricot Bars

1¼ cups plain (all-purpose) flour	**300 ml**
¾ cup brown sugar	**180 ml**
6 tablespoons butter	**90 ml**
¾ cup apricot jam (jelly)	**180 ml**

- Preheat oven to 180° C (350° F).
- In mixing bowl, combine flour, brown sugar and butter and mix well.
- Place half mixture in 23-cm (9-inch) square baking pan, spread apricot jam (jelly) over top and sprinkle with remaining flour mixture. Bake for 30 minutes. Cut into squares.

Walnut Bars

1⅔ cups shredded wheatmeal biscuit (cracker) crumbs	400 ml
1½ cups walnuts, coarsely chopped	360 ml
1 (14 ounce) can sweetened condensed milk	395 g
¼ cup flaked coconut, optional	60 ml

- Preheat oven to 180° C (350° F). Place biscuit (cracker) crumbs and walnuts in bowl.
- Slowly add sweetened condensed milk, coconut and a dash of salt. (Mixture will be very thick.) Pack into sprayed 23-cm (9-inch) square pan and press mixture down with back of spoon.
- Bake for 35 minutes and cut into squares when cool.

Pecan Squares

1 (24 ounce) package white almond bark	680 g
1 cup white chocolate chips	240 ml
1 teaspoon cinnamon	5 ml
1 cup pecans, chopped	240 ml
8 cups frosted rice crispy cereal	1.8 L

- Melt almond bark, chocolate chips and cinnamon in very large saucepan or roasting pan on low heat and stir constantly until they melt.
- Remove from heat and add pecans and cereal. Mix well and stir into 23 x 33-cm (9 x 13-inch) pan. Pat down with back of spoon, refrigerate just until set and cut into squares.

Chinese Cookies

1 (6 ounce) package butterscotch chips	170 g
1 (6 ounce) package chocolate chips	170 g
2 cups chow mein noodles	480 ml
1¼ cups salted peanuts	300 ml

- On low heat, melt butterscotch and chocolate chips. Add noodles and peanuts and mix well.
- Drop by teaspoonfuls onto greaseproof (wax) paper and refrigerate to harden.
- Store in airtight container.

Butterscotch Cookies

18 ounce butterscotch chips	340 g
2¼ cups chow mein noodles	540 ml
½ cup walnuts, chopped	120 ml
¼ cup flaked coconut	60 ml

- Melt butterscotch chips in bain-marie (double boiler). Add noodles, walnuts and coconut.
- Drop by tablespoonfuls onto greaseproof (wax) paper and refrigerate to harden.
- Store in airtight container.

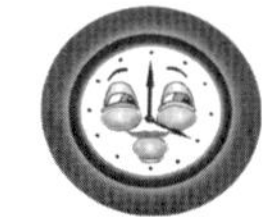

Coconut Yummies

1 (12 ounce) package white chocolate baking chips	340 g
¼ cup butter	60 ml
16 large marshmallows	
2 cups quick-cooking oats	480 ml
1 cup flaked coconut	240 ml

- In saucepan over low heat, melt chocolate chips, butter and marshmallows and stir until smooth.
- Stir in oats and coconut and mix well.
- Drop by rounded teaspoonfuls onto greaseproof (wax) paper-lined baking trays (sheets).
- Chill until set and store in airtight container.

Haystacks

1 (12 ounce) package butterscotch chips	340 g
1 cup salted peanuts	240 ml
1½ cups chow mein noodles	360 ml

- Melt butterscotch chips in top of bain-marie (double boiler).
- Remove from heat and stir in peanuts and noodles.
- Drop by teaspoonfuls onto greaseproof (wax) paper.
- Cool and store in airtight container.

Orange Balls

12 ounce vanilla biscuits (wafers), crushed	340 g
½ cup butter, melted	120 ml
1 (16 ounce) box icing (confectioner's) sugar	.5 kg
1 (6 ounce) can orange juice cordial (concentrate)	170 g
1 cup pecans, finely chopped	240 ml

- Combine biscuit (wafer) crumbs, butter, sugar and orange juice cordial (concentrate) and mix well.
- Form into balls, roll in chopped pecans and store in airtight container.
- Make these in finger shapes for something different. They make great cookies for a party or afternoon tea.

Peanut Butter Crunchies

1 cup sugar	240 ml
½ cup white glucose (corn) syrup	120 ml
2 cups peanut butter	480 ml
4 cups rice crispy cereal	1 L

- In saucepan, mix sugar and syrup and bring to a rolling boil.
- Remove from stove and stir in peanut butter. Add cereal and mix well.
- Drop by teaspoonfuls onto greaseproof (wax) paper and place in refrigerator for a few minutes to set.

Scotch Shortbread

½ cup unsalted butter, softened	120 ml
⅓ cup sugar	80 ml
1¼ cups plain (all-purpose) flour	300 ml
Icing (confectioner's) sugar	

- Preheat oven to 160° C (325° F).
- Cream butter and sugar until light and fluffy. Add flour and a dash of salt and mix well.
- Spread dough into 20-cm (8-inch) square pan and bake for 20 minutes or until light brown. Let shortbread cool in pan, dust with icing (powdered) sugar and cut into squares.

Sand Tarts

1 cup butter, softened	240 ml
¾ cup icing (confectioner's) sugar	180 ml
2 cups sifted plain (all-purpose) flour	480 ml
1 cup pecans, chopped	240 ml
1 teaspoon vanilla extract	5 ml

- Preheat oven to 160° C (325° F).
- With mixer, cream butter and sugar and add flour, pecans and vanilla.
- Roll into crescents and place on unsprayed baking tray (sheet). Bake for 20 minutes and roll in extra sugar after tarts cool.

Pecan Puffs

2 egg whites	
¾ cup light brown sugar	180 ml
1 teaspoon vanilla extract	5 ml
1 cup pecans, chopped	240 ml

- Preheat oven to 120° C (250° F).
- Beat egg whites until foamy and add brown sugar ¼ cup (60 ml) at a time.
- Add vanilla, continue beating until stiff peaks form (about 3 or 4 minutes) and fold in pecans.
- Line baking tray (sheet) with freezer paper and drop mixture by teaspoonfuls onto paper.
- Bake for 45 minutes.

Coconut Macaroons

2 (7 ounce) packages flaked coconut	2 (200 g)
1 (14 ounce) can sweetened condensed milk	395 g
2 teaspoons vanilla extract	10 ml
½ teaspoon almond extract	2 ml

- Preheat oven to 180° C (350° F). In mixing bowl, combine coconut, sweetened condensed milk and extracts and mix well.
- Drop by rounded teaspoonfuls onto foil-lined baking tray (sheet). Bake for 8 to 10 minutes or until light brown around edges.
- Immediately remove from foil. (Macaroons will stick if allowed to cool.) Store at room temperature.

Butter Cookies

1 pound butter	.5 kg
¾ cup brown sugar	180 ml
¾ cup white (granulated) sugar	180 ml
4½ cups plain (all-purpose) flour	1.1 L

- Preheat oven to 180° C (350° F). Cream butter and sugars, slowly add flour and mix well. (Batter will be very thick.)
- Roll into small balls and place on unsprayed baking tray (sheet). Bake for about 15 minutes until only slightly brown. (Do not overbake.)

Chocolate Mud Cookies

1 (18 ounce) box chocolate mud cake mix 510 g
½ cup oil 120 ml
2 eggs
¾ cup pecans, chopped, optional 180 ml

- Preheat oven to 180° C (350° F).
- Combine cake mix, oil and eggs in bowl and mix well. (If you like, fold in chopped pecans.)
- Drop by teaspoonfuls onto non-stick baking tray (sheet).
- Bake for 10 to 12 minutes. Cool and remove to wire rack.

Brown Sugar Cookies

¾ cup brown sugar 180 ml
1 cup butter, softened 240 ml
1 egg yolk
2 cups plain (all-purpose) flour 480 ml

- Cream sugar and butter until light and fluffy.
- Mix in egg yolk and blend in flour. Refrigerate dough for 1 hour.
- Form dough into 2.5-cm (1-inch) balls, flatten and criss-cross with fork on lightly sprayed baking tray (sheet).
- Bake at 160° C (325° F) for 10 to 12 minutes or until golden brown.

Cherry Crisp

2 (20 ounce) cans pitted cherries	2 (565 g)
1 (18 ounce) box white cake mix	510 g
½ cup butter	120 ml
2 cups pecans, chopped	480 ml

- Preheat oven to 180° C (350° F).
- Pour cherries into sprayed 23 x 33-cm (9 x 13-inch) baking dish. Sprinkle cake mix over top.
- Dot with butter and cover with pecans. Bake uncovered for 45 minutes.

Blueberry Crunch

1 (20 ounce) can crushed pineapple with juice	565 g
1 (18 ounce) box yellow cake mix	510 g
3 cups fresh or frozen blueberries	710 ml
⅔ cup sugar	160 ml
½ cup butter, melted	120 ml

- Preheat oven to 180° C (350° F).
- Spread pineapple in sprayed 23 x 33-cm (9 x 13-inch) baking dish and sprinkle cake mix, blueberries and sugar over top.
- Drizzle with butter and bake for 45 minutes or until bubbly.

Apricot Cobbler

So easy and so good!

1 (20 ounce) can apricot halves	565 g
1 (20 ounce) can crushed pineapple with juice	565 g
1 cup pecans, chopped	240 ml
1 (18 ounce) box yellow cake mix	510 g
1 cup butter, melted	240 ml

- Preheat oven to 190° C (375° F).
- Spray 23 x 33-cm (9 x 13-inch) baking dish. Pour apricots in pan and spread out.
- Spoon pineapple and juice over apricots and sprinkle pecans over pineapple.
- Sprinkle cake mix over pecans.
- Drizzle melted butter over cake mix and bake for 40 minutes or until light brown and crunchy.
- Serve hot or at room temperature. It's great topped with whipped cream (topping).

Cherry Cobbler

2 (20 ounce) cans pitted cherries	2 (565 g)
1 (18 ounce) box white cake mix	510 g
¾ cup butter, melted	180 ml
1 (4 ounce) package almonds, slivered	115 g

- Preheat oven to 180° C (350° F).
- Spread cherries in sprayed 23 x 33-cm (9 x 13-inch) baking pan. Sprinkle cake mix over cherries, drizzle with melted butter and sprinkle almonds over top.
- Bake for 45 minutes. Top with whipped cream (topping).

Easy Pumpkin Pie

2 eggs	
3 cups cooked, mashed pumpkin	720 g
¼ teaspoon nutmeg	1 ml
1 (5 ounce) can evaporated milk	145 g
1 (9 inch) deep-dish piecrust	23 cm

- Preheat oven to 200° C (400° F).
- Beat eggs lightly in large bowl and stir in pumpkin, nutmeg and evaporated milk. Pour into piecrust. (Cover piecrust edges with strips of foil to prevent excessive browning.)
- Bake for 15 minutes. Reduce temperature to 160° C (325° F) and bake for additional 40 minutes or until knife inserted in centre comes out clean and cool.

Black Forest Pie

This is definitely a party dessert, but the family will insist it should be served on a regular basis.

4 (1 ounce) squares unsweetened baking chocolate	**4 (30 g)**
1 (14 ounce) can sweetened condensed milk	**395 g**
1 teaspoon almond extract	**5 ml**
1½ cups thickened (whipping) cream, whipped	**360 ml**
1 (9 inch) prepared piecrust	**23 cm**
1 (20 ounce) can pitted cherries, chilled	**565 g**

- In saucepan over medium-low heat, melt chocolate with sweetened condensed milk and stir well to mix.
- Remove from heat and stir in extract. (This mixture needs to cool.)
- When mixture is about room temperature, pour chocolate into whipped cream and fold gently until they combine.
- Pour into piecrust.
- To serve, spoon heaping spoonful of cherries over each piece of pie.

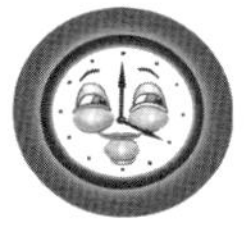

Do not keep chocolate in the refrigerator.
It is best stored between 15° and 21° C (60° and 70° F).

Easy Chocolate Pie

1 (8 ounce) milk chocolate (candy) bar	225 g
1 (16 ounce) carton whipped cream (topping), divided	.5 kg
¾ cup pecans, chopped	180 ml
1 (9 inch) prepared piecrust	23 cm

- In saucepan, break chocolate into small pieces and melt over low heat. Remove and cool several minutes.
- Fold in two-thirds whipped cream (topping), mix well and stir in chopped pecans. Pour into piecrust, spread remaining whipped cream over top and chill for at least 8 hours.

Dixie Pie

24 large marshmallows	
1 cup evaporated milk	240 ml
1 (8 ounce) carton thickened (whipping) cream, whipped	225 g
3 tablespoons bourbon	45 ml
1 (6 ounce) chocolate piecrust	170 g

- In saucepan on low heat, melt marshmallows in milk and stir constantly. (Do not boil.) Cool in refrigerator.
- Fold into cream while adding bourbon and pour into piecrust. Refrigerate at least 5 hours before serving.

Chess Pie

½ cup butter, softened	120 ml
2 cups sugar	480 ml
1 tablespoon cornflour (cornstarch)	15 ml
4 eggs	
1 (9 inch) piecrust	23 cm

- Preheat oven to 160° C (325° F).
- Cream butter, sugar and cornflour (cornstarch). Add eggs one at a time and beat well after each addition.
- Pour mixture into piecrust. (Cover piecrust edges with strips of foil to prevent excessive browning.)
- Bake for 45 minutes or until centre sets.

Peanut Butter Pie

⅔ cup crunchy peanut butter	160 ml
1 (8 ounce) package cream cheese, softened	225 g
½ cup milk	120 ml
1 cup icing (powdered) sugar	240 ml
1 (8 ounce) carton whipped cream (topping)	225 g
1 (9 ounce) wheatmeal piecrust	255 g

- With mixer, blend peanut butter, cream cheese, milk and sugar and fold in whipped cream (topping).
- Pour into piecrust and refrigerate several hours.

Peach-Mousse Pie

Incredibly good!

16 ounce peach slices	.5 kg
1 cup sugar	240 ml
1 (1 ounce) packet unflavoured gelatine	30 g
⅛ teaspoon ground nutmeg	.5 ml
6 ounce whipped cream (topping)	170 g
1 (9 ounce) wheatmeal piecrust	255 g

- Place peaches in blender and process until smooth.
- Transfer peaches to saucepan, bring to a boil and stir constantly.
- Combine sugar, gelatine and nutmeg and stir into hot puree until sugar and gelatine dissolve.
- Pour gelatine-peach mixture into large mixing bowl.
- Place in freezer until mixture mounds (about 20 minutes) and stir occasionally.
- Beat mixture at high speed about 5 minutes until it becomes light and frothy.
- Fold in whipped cream (topping) and spoon into piecrust.

Strawberry-Cream Cheese Pie

20 ounce strawberries	570 g
2 (8 ounce) packages cream cheese, softened	2 (225 g)
⅔ cup icing (powdered) sugar	160 ml
1 (8 ounce) carton whipped cream (topping)	225 g
1 (6 ounce) chocolate crumb piecrust	170 g

- Chop strawberries into quarters.
- In mixing bowl, combine cream cheese, strawberries and sugar and beat well.
- Fold in whipped cream (topping) and spoon into piecrust.
- Refrigerate overnight and garnish with fresh strawberries.

Creamy Lemon Pie

1 (8 ounce) package cream cheese, softened	225 g
1 (14 ounce) can sweetened condensed milk	395 g
¼ cup lemon juice	60 ml
1 (20 ounce) can lemon pie filling (or lemon curd)	565 g
1 (9 ounce) wheatmeal piecrust	255 g

- In mixing bowl, beat cream cheese until creamy.
- Add sweetened condensed milk and lemon juice and beat until mixture is very creamy.
- Fold in custard powder, stir until creamy and pour into piecrust.
- Refrigerate several hours before slicing and serving.

Limeade Pie

6 ounces lime juice cordial (concentrate)	170 g
2 cups low-fat frozen yoghurt, softened	480 ml
1 (8 ounce) carton whipped cream (topping)	225 g
1 (6 ounce) wheatmeal piecrust	170 g

- In large mixing bowl, combine lime cordial (concentrate) and yoghurt and mix well.
- Fold in whipped cream (topping) and pour into piecrust.
- Freeze for at least 4 hours or overnight.

Easy Cheesecake

2 (8 ounce) packages cream cheese, softened	2 (225 g)
½ cup sugar	120 ml
½ teaspoon vanilla extract	2 ml
2 eggs	
1 (9 ounce) wheatmeal piecrust	255 g

- Preheat oven to 180° C (350° F).
- In mixing bowl, beat cream cheese, sugar, vanilla essence and eggs and pour into piecrust.
- Bake for 40 minutes.
- Cool and top with any flavour jam (jelly).

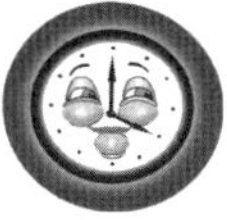

When you need a dessert in a hurry, buy a cheesecake and pour jam (jelly) over the top.

Old-Fashioned Apple Sauce Spice Cake

1 (18 ounce) box spice cake mix	510 g
3 eggs	
1¼ cups apple sauce	300 ml
⅓ cup oil	80 ml
1 cup pecans, chopped	240 ml

- Preheat oven to 180° C (350° F).
- With mixer, combine cake mix, eggs, apple sauce and oil and beat at medium speed for 2 minutes.
- Stir in pecans and pour into sprayed, floured 23 x 33-cm (9 x 13-inch) baking pan.
- Bake for 40 minutes or until toothpick inserted near centre comes out clean. Cool.
- For icing (frosting), use prepared vanilla icing and add ½ teaspoon (2 ml) cinnamon.

Lemon-Pineapple Cake

1 (18 ounce) carton lemon cake mix	**510 g**
1 (20 ounce) can crushed pineapple with juice	**565 g**
3 eggs	
⅓ cup oil	**80 ml**

- Preheat oven to 180° C (350° F).
- In mixing bowl, combine all cake ingredients. Blend on low speed to moisten and beat on medium for 2 minutes.
- Pour batter into sprayed, floured 23 x 33-cm (9 x 13-inch) baking pan.
- Bake for 30 minutes. Cake is done when toothpick inserted in centre comes out clean. (While cake is baking, prepare topping.) Cool for 15 minutes.

Lemon-Pineapple Cake Topping:

1 (14 ounce) can sweetened condensed milk	**395 g**
1 cup sour cream	**240 ml**
¼ cup lemon juice	**60 ml**

- In medium bowl, combine all topping ingredients. Stir well to blend.
- Pour over warm cake. Chill.

Hawaiian Dream Cake

This is a wonderful cake!

1 (18 ounce) carton yellow cake mix	**510 g**
4 eggs	
¾ cup oil	**180 ml**
½ (20 ounce) can crushed pineapple with half juice	**½ (565 g)**

- Preheat oven to 180° C (350° F).
- With mixer, beat all ingredients for 4 minutes. Pour into sprayed, floured 23 x 33-cm (9 x 13-inch) baking pan.
- Bake for 30 to 35 minutes or until toothpick inserted in centre comes out clean. Cool and spread Coconut-Pineapple Icing over cake.

Coconut-Pineapple Icing (Frosting):

½ (20 ounce) can crushed pineapple with half juice	**½ (565 g)**
½ cup butter	**120 ml**
16 ounce icing (confectioner's) sugar	**.5 kg**
6 ounce flaked coconut	**170 g**

- Heat pineapple and butter and boil for 2 minutes. Add sugar and coconut.
- Punch holes in cake with knife and pour hot icing over cake.

Two-Surprise Cake

The first surprise is how easy it is to make and the second surprise is how good it is! You'll make this more than once.

1 bakery orange cake	
1 (15 ounce) can crushed pineapple with juice	**425 g**
1 (3.4 ounce) package instant vanilla pudding mix	**100 g**
1 (8 ounce) carton whipped cream (topping)	**225 g**
½ cup slivered almonds, toasted	**120 ml**

- Slice cake horizontally into 3 equal layers.
- Mix pineapple, pudding mix and whipped cream (topping) and blend well.
- Spread pineapple mixture onto each cake layer and top of cake. Sprinkle almonds on top and chill.

Strawberry Sponge Cake

1 (18 ounce) carton strawberry cake mix	510 g
1 (3.4 ounce) package instant strawberry pudding mix	100 g
⅓ cup oil	80 ml
4 eggs	
1 (3 ounce) package strawberry gelatine	85 g

- Preheat oven to 160° C (325° F).
- Mix all ingredients plus 1 cup (240 ml) water and beat for 2 minutes at medium speed.
- Pour into sprayed, floured bundt pan.
- Bake for 55 to 60 minutes. Cake is done when toothpick inserted near centre comes out clean.
- Cool for 20 minutes before removing cake from pan. If you would like an icing, use commercial vanilla icing.

TIP: If you like coconut better than pineapple, use coconut cream pudding mix instead of pineapple.

Coconut Cake Deluxe

This is a fabulous cake!

1 (18 ounce) carton yellow cake mix	**510 g**
1 (14 ounce) can sweetened condensed milk	**396 g**
1 (15 ounce) can coconut cream	**425 g**
1 (3 ounce) packet flaked coconut	**85 g**
1 (8 ounce) carton whipped cream (topping)	**225 g**

- Preheat oven to 180° C (350° F).
- Mix cake batter according to package directions.
- Pour batter into sprayed, floured 23 x 33-cm (9 x 13-inch) baking pan and bake for 30 to 35 minutes or until toothpick inserted in centre comes out clean.
- While cake is warm, punch holes in cake about 5 cm (2 inches) apart.
- Pour sweetened condensed milk over cake and spread until all milk soaks into cake.
- Pour coconut cream over cake and sprinkle with coconut.
- Cool, frost with whipped cream (topping) and chill.

Chocolate Cookie Cake

1 (18 ounce) box white cake mix	510 g
⅓ cup oil	80 ml
4 egg whites	
1¼ cup chocolate biscuits (cookies), coarsely chopped	300 ml

- Preheat oven to 180° C (350° F). In mixing bowl, combine cake mix, oil, egg whites and 1¼ cups (300 ml) water.
- Blend on low speed until moist and then beat for 2 minutes at high speed. Gently fold in coarsely chopped biscuits (cookies) and pour batter into 2 sprayed, floured 20-cm (8-inch) round cake pans.
- Bake for 25 to 30 minutes or until toothpick inserted in centre comes out clean. Cool for 15 minutes and remove from pan. Cool completely and ice (frost).

Chocolate Cookie Cake Icing (Frosting):

4¼ cups icing (powdered) sugar	1.1 L
1 cup butter, softened	240 ml
1 cup shortening	240 ml
1 teaspoon almond extract	5 ml
½ cup chocolate biscuits (cookies), crushed	120 ml

- With mixer, combine all icing (frosting) ingredients and beat until creamy. Ice first layer of cake, place second layer on top and frost top and sides. Sprinkle biscuit (cookie) crumbs over top.
- Do not use butter-flavoured shortening.

Chocolate-Cherry Cake

This is a chocolate lover's dream.

1 (18 ounce) carton milk chocolate cake mix — 510 g
1 (20 ounce) can pitted cherries — 565 g
3 eggs

- Preheat oven to 180° C (350° F).
- In mixing bowl, combine cake mix, cherries and eggs.
- Mix by hand and pour into sprayed, floured 23 x 33-cm (9 x 13-inch) baking dish.
- Bake for 35 to 40 minutes. Cake is done when toothpick inserted in centre comes out clean.

Chocolate-Cherry Cake Icing (Frosting):

5 tablespoons butter — 75 ml
1¼ cups sugar — 300 ml
½ cup milk — 120 ml
1 (6 ounce) package chocolate chips — 170 g

- When cake is done, combine butter, sugar and milk in medium saucepan.
- Boil 1 minute and stir constantly.
- Add chocolate chips and stir until chips melt.
- Pour over hot cake.

Cream Cake Dessert

1 bakery layered cream sponge (pound cake)	
4 bananas, sliced	
1 (5 ounce) package instant vanilla pudding mix	145 g
1 (20 ounce) can crushed pineapple, drained	565 g
1 (8 ounce) carton whipped cream (topping)	225 g

- Slice sponge (pound) cake and place in sprayed 23 x 33-cm (9 x 13-inch) pan cream-side up.
- Make layer of sliced bananas.
- Prepare pudding according to package directions (use 2 cups/480 ml milk).
- Pour pudding over bananas and add pineapple.
- Top with whipped cream (topping) and refrigerate.
- Cut into squares to serve.

Sometimes the simplest of ideas will make the best desserts. If you're hungry for something sweet or have unexpected guests, you can't go wrong with canned fruit poured over ready-made cake and topped with whipped cream (topping).

Strawberry Trifle

1 (5 ounce) package instant vanilla pudding mix	145 g
1 (12 ounce) prepared bakery sponge (pound) cake, sliced	340 g
2 cups fresh strawberries, sliced	480 ml
½ cup sherry	120 ml
Whipped cream (topping)	

- Prepare pudding according to package directions.
- Place layer of cake slices in 20-cm (8-inch) crystal bowl and sprinkle with ¼ cup (60 ml) sherry.
- Layer half of strawberries and half pudding on top.
- Repeat all layers and chill overnight or several hours.
- Before serving, top with whipped cream (topping).

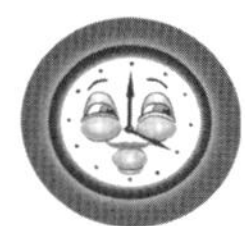

Peachy Sundaes

1 pint vanilla ice-cream	.5 kg
¾ cup peach jam (jelly), warmed	180 ml
¼ cup chopped almonds, toasted	180 ml
¼ cup flaked coconut	180 ml

- Divide ice-cream into 4 sherbet dishes.
- Top with jam (jelly).
- Sprinkle with almonds and coconut.

Mango Cream

2 soft mangoes	
½ gallon vanilla ice-cream, softened	2 L
6 ounce lemon juice cordial (concentrate)	170 g
1 (8 ounce) carton whipped cream (topping)	225 g

- Peel mangoes, cut slices around seeds and cut into small chunks.
- In large bowl, mix ice-cream, cordial (concentrate) and whipped cream (topping) and fold in mango chunks.
- Quickly spoon mixture into parfait or sherbet glasses and cover with cling (plastic) wrap.
- Place in freezer.

Butterscotch Finale

1 (16 ounce) carton thickened (whipping) cream	.5 kg
¾ cup butterscotch ice-cream topping	180 ml
1 (14 ounce) prepared angel food cake	395 g
¾ pound toffee bars, crushed, divided	340 g

- In mixing bowl, whip cream until thick. Slowly add butterscotch topping and beat until mixture is thick.
- Slice cake horizontally into 3 equal layers.
- Place bottom layer on cake plate, spread with 1½ cups (360 ml) whipped cream mixture and sprinkle with one-fourth crushed toffee.
- Repeat layers and ice (frost) top and sides of cake with remaining whipped cream mixture.
- Sprinkle toffee over top of cake. Chill for at least 8 hours before serving.

Keeping an angel food cake in the freezer will make you look like a kitchen pro when it comes time to prepare a last-minute dessert. You can top cake with fresh berries, canned fruit, ice-cream, chocolate syrup, butterscotch syrup or caramel sauce, and always whipped cream (topping).

Ice-Cream Dessert

18 ice-cream sandwiches	
1 (12 ounce) carton whipped cream (topping)	340 g
1 (12 ounce) jar hot fudge ice-cream topping	340 g
1 cup salted peanuts	240 ml

- Cut 1 ice-cream sandwich in half.
- Place 1 whole and 1 half sandwich along short side of unsprayed 23 x 33-cm (9 x 13-inch) pan.
- Arrange 8 sandwiches in opposite direction in pan.
- Spread with half whipped cream (topping).
- Spoon fudge topping by teaspoonfuls onto topping and sprinkle with ½ cup (120 ml) peanuts.
- Repeat layers with remaining ice-cream sandwiches, topping and peanuts. (Pan will be full.)
- Cover and freeze. Take out of freezer 20 minutes before serving.

When you need a dessert fast, try ice-cream with liqueur poured over it. Keep a bottle of almond-flavoured liqueur (Amaretto®), coffee-flavoured liqueur (Kahlua®), raspberry-flavoured liqueur (Chambord®) or your favourite flavoured drink. It's so fast and easy! And it tastes really special.

Blueberry-Angel Dessert

1 (8 ounce) package cream cheese, softened	225 g
1 cup icing (confectioner's) sugar	240 ml
1 (8 ounce) carton whipped cream (topping)	225 g
1 (14 ounce) prepared bakery angel food cake	395 g
40 ounce canned blueberries	1.15 kg

- In large mixing bowl, beat cream cheese and icing (powdered) sugar and fold in whipped cream (topping).
- Tear cake into small 2.5-cm (1 or 2-inch) cubes and fold into cream cheese mixture.
- Spread mixture evenly in 23 x 33-cm (9 x 13-inch) dish and top with blueberries.
- Cover and refrigerate for at least 3 hours before cutting into squares to serve.

Blueberry Fluff

20 ounce canned blueberries	**565 g**
1 (20 ounce) can crushed pineapple, drained	**565 g**
1 (14 ounce) can sweetened condensed milk	**395 g**
1 (8 ounce) carton whipped cream (topping)	**225 g**

- Mix blueberries, pineapple and sweetened condensed milk.
- Fold in whipped cream (topping). (This dessert is even better if you add ¾ cup/180 ml chopped pecans.)
- Pour into parfait glasses and chill.

Brandied Fruit

40 ounce canned crushed pineapple	**1.15 kg**
16 ounce canned sliced peaches	**.5 kg**
22 ounce mandarine pieces (tidbits)	**625 g**
1 (10 ounce) jar glacé (maraschino) cherries	**280 g**
Sugar	
1 cup brandy	**240 ml**

- Let all fruit drain for 12 hours.
- For every cup of drained fruit, add ½ cup (120 ml) sugar. Let stand 12 hours.
- Add brandy, spoon into large jar and store in refrigerator. This mixture needs to stand in refrigerator for 3 weeks.
- Serve over ice-cream.

Fun Fruit Fajitas

1 (20 ounce) can pitted cherries	**565 g**
8 large flour tortillas	
1½ cups sugar	**360 ml**
¾ cup butter	**180 ml**
1 teaspoon almond essence (flavouring)	**5 ml**

- Divide fruit equally on tortillas, roll and place in 23 x 33-cm (9 x 13-inch) baking dish.
- Mix sugar and butter in saucepan with 2 cups (480 ml) water and bring to a boil.
- Add almond essence (flavouring) and pour sugar mixture over flour tortillas.
- Place in refrigerator and soak 1 to 24 hours.
- Bake at 180° C (350° F) for 20 minutes or until brown and bubbly. Serve hot or at room temperature.

TIP: Use any flavour of canned fruit you like.

Amaretto Peaches

4½ cups peeled, sliced fresh peaches	1.1 L
½ cup Amaretto® liqueur	120 ml
½ cup sour cream	120 ml
½ cup brown sugar	120 ml

- Lay peaches in 2-L (2-quart) baking dish.
- Pour Amaretto® over peaches and spread with sour cream.
- Sprinkle brown sugar evenly over top.
- Grill (broil) mixture until it heats thoroughly and sugar melts.
- Serve over ice-cream or pound cake.

Amaretto Ice-Cream

1 (8 ounce) carton thickened (whipping) cream, whipped	225 g
1 pint vanilla ice-cream, softened	.5 kg
⅓ cup Amaretto® liqueur	80 ml
⅓ cup almonds, chopped, toasted	80 ml

- Combine cream, ice-cream and Amaretto® and freeze in sherbet glasses.
- When ready to serve, drizzle a little additional Amaretto over top of each individual serving and sprinkle with toasted almonds.

Measurements & Conversions

3 teaspoons	1 tablespoon		
4 tablespoons	¼ cup	2 fluid ounces	60 ml
8 tablespoons	½ cup	4 fluid ounces	120 ml
12 tablespoons	¾ cup	6 fluid ounces	180 ml
16 tablespoons	1 cup	8 fluid ounces	240 ml
¼ cup	4 tablespoons	2 fluid ounces	60 ml
⅓ cup	5 tablespoons + 1 teaspoon		80 ml
½ cup	8 tablespoons	4 fluid ounces	120 ml
⅔ cup	10 tablespoons + 2 teaspoons		160 ml
¾ cup	12 tablespoons	6 fluid ounces	180 ml
1 cup	16 tablespoons	8 fluid ounces	240 ml
1 cup	½ pint		
2 cups	1 pint	16 fluid ounces	480 ml
3 cups	1½ pints	24 fluid ounces	720 ml
4 cups	1 quart	32 fluid ounces	1 L
8 cups	2 quarts	64 fluid ounces	2 L
1 pint	2 cups	16 fluid ounces	480 ml
2 pints	1 quart		1 L
1 quart	2 pints; 4 cups	32 fluid ounces	1 L
4 quarts	1 gallon; 8 pints; 16 cups		4 L
8 quarts	1 peck		8 L
4 pecks	1 bushel		32 L

Cake Pans

5 x 2 round	2⅔ cups
6 x 2 round	3¾ cups
8 x 1.5 round	4 cups
7 x 2 round	5¼ cups
8 x 2 round	6 cups
9 x 1.5 round	6 cups
9 x 2 round	8 cups
9 x 3 bundt	9 cups
10 x 3.5 bundt	12 cups
9.5 x 2.5 springform	10 cups
10 x 2.5 springform	12 cups
8 x 3 tube	9 cups
9 x 4 tube	11 cups
10 x 4 tube	16 cups

Casserole Dishes

8 x 8 x 12 square	8 cups
11 x 7 x 12 rectangular	8 cups
9 x 9 x 2 square	10 cups
13 x 9 x 2 rectangular	15 cups
1-quart casserole	4 cups
2-quart casserole	8 cups
2.5 quart casserole	10 cups
3-quart casserole	12 cups

Quick Tip

Stock up with partly baked breads and pastries; prepared ready-to-serve meals and pasta dishes; milk, cream, and whipped desserts.

Shopping List for Busy Woman's Quick 'n Easy

Pantry Staples

Baking cocoa
Baking powder
Bicarbonate of soda (baking soda)
Black pepper
Canola oil
Cayenne pepper
Chicken stock (bouillon)
Chilli powder
Cider vinegar
Cornflour (cornstarch)
Dried basil
Dried oregano
Ground mustard
Honey
Icing (confectioner's) sugar
Olive oil
Peanut butter
Plain (all-purpose) flour
Polenta (cornmeal)
Red wine vinegar
Soy sauce
Salt
Sugar
Vanilla extract
White pepper

Fresh Produce

___ Apples
___ Avocados
___ Bananas
___ Beans
___ Broccoli
___ Cabbage
___ Capsicums (Peppers)
___ Carrots
___ Cauliflower
___ Celery
___ Chillies
___ Corn
___ Cucumbers
___ Garlic
___ Grapefruit
___ Grapes
___ Lemons
___ Lettuce
___ Lime
___ Melons
___ Mushrooms
___ Onions
___ Oranges
___ Peaches
___ Pears
___ Potatoes
___ Pumpkin
___ Strawberries
___ Spinach
___ Tomatoes
___ Zucchini (Courgettes)
___ ____________
___ ____________

Deli

___ Cheese
___ Chicken
___ Turkey
___ Ham
___ Main Dish
___ Prepared Salad
___ Sandwich Meat
___ Side Dish
___ ____________

Fresh Bakery

___ Bagels
___ Bread
___ Cake
___ Croissants
___ Doughnuts
___ French Stick (Bread)
___ Muffins
___ Pastries
___ Pies
___ Rolls

Dairy

___ Butter
___ Cheese
___ Cottage Cheese
___ Cream Cheese
___ Cream
___ Eggs
___ Juice
___ Margarine
___ Milk
___ Pudding
___ Sour Cream
___ Yoghurt
___ ____________
___ ____________

Frozen Foods

___ Breakfast
___ Dinners
___ Ice
___ Ice-Cream
___ Juice
___ Pastries
___ Pies
___ Pizza
___ Potatoes
___ Unthickened (Half and Half) Cream
___ Vegetables
___ Whipped Cream (Topping)

Grocery List for Busy Woman's Quick'n Easy

Grocery

___ Beans
___ Beer/Wine
___ Biscuits (Crackers)
___ Bread
___ Canned Vegetables
___ ______________
___ ______________
___ Cereal
___ Chips/Snacks
___ Coffee
___ Cookies
___ Cordial (Concentrate)
___ Flour
___ Honey
___ Jam (Jelly)
___ Juice
___ Mayonnaise
___ Mixes
___ ______________
___ ______________
___ Mustard
___ Nuts/Seeds
___ Oil
___ Pasta
___ Peanut Butter
___ Pickles/Olives
___ Popcorn
___ Rice
___ Salad Dressing
___ Salt
___ Seasonings
___ ______________
___ ______________
___ Soft drinks
___ Soups
___ Spices
___ ______________
___ ______________
___ Sugar
___ Syrup
___ Tea
___ Tomato Sauce (Ketchup)
___ Tortillas
___ Water
___ ______________
___ ______________

Meat

___ Bacon
___ Beef Mince (Ground Beef)
___ Chicken
___ Ham
___ Hot Dogs
___ Pork
___ Roast
___ Sandwich Meat
___ Sausage
___ Steak
___ Turkey
___ ______________
___ ______________

General Merchandise

___ Automotive
___ Baby Items
___ ______________
___ Bath Soap
___ Deodorant
___ Detergent
___ Dish Soap
___ Facial Tissue
___ Feminine Products
___ Aluminium Foil
___ Greeting Cards
___ Hardware
___ Insecticides
___ Light Bulbs
___ Lotion
___ Medicine
___ Napkins
___ Paper Plates
___ Paper Towels
___ Pet Supplies
___ Prescriptions
___ Shampoo
___ Toothpaste
___ Vitamins
___ ______________
___ ______________

Quick Tip

Keep a supply of whole and chopped tomatoes and beans; vegetables such as corn, asparagus and artichoke hearts; tuna; cooked ham; sauces; condensed and ready-to-heat soups; peanut and other nut butters.

Food Substitutions

You Need:	Use Instead:
1 cup breadcrumbs	¾ cup biscuit (cracker) crumbs
1 cup butter	⅞ cup vegetable oil or shortening
1 cup buttermilk	1 cup whole milk plus 1 tablespoon vinegar or lemon juice; or 1 cup plain yoghurt
1 ounce unsweetened chocolate	3 tablespoons unsweetened cocoa plus 1 tablespoon butter
1 tablespoon cornflour	2 tablespoons plain (all-purpose) flour
1 cup biscuit (cracker) crumbs	1¼ cups breadcrumbs
1 cup cake flour	1 cup, less 2 tablespoons plain (all-purpose) flour
1 clove garlic	1 teaspoon garlic salt less ½ teaspoon salt in recipe
1 tablespoon fresh herbs	1 teaspoon dried herbs
1 cup milk	½ cup evaporated milk plus ½ cup water; or ¾ cup low fat milk plus ¼ cup butter
1 tablespoon prepared mustard	1 teaspoon dry mustard
1 small onion	1 tablespoon minced onion; or ½ teaspoon onion powder
1 cup sour cream	1 cup plain yoghurt; or 1 tablespoon lemon juice plus enough evaporated whole milk to equal 1 cup
1 cup sugar	1¾ cups icing (powdered) sugar; or 1 cup packed brown sugar
1 cup icing (confectioner's) sugar	½ cup plus 1 tablespoon white (granulated) sugar
1 cup tomato juice	½ cup tomato sauce plus ½ cup water
1 cup tomato sauce	½ cup tomato paste plus ½ cup water
1 cup yoghurt	1 cup milk plus 1 tablespoon lemon juice

Quick Tip

Stock sauce and gravy mixes; dried vegetables; instant mashed potatoes, pasta and rice mixes; instant desserts; dried milk and gelatine powder; bread, pastry, batter and cake mixes. Keep jams (jellies); fruits in brandy; ready-made meals such as chilli con carne or baked beans; pesto; olives; sun-dried tomatoes; and antipasto.

Index

D

E

M

N

O

P

T